TREASURY·OF
CROSS-STITCH SAMPLERS

▪ ▪ ▪ ▪ ▪

Sharon Perna

Sterling Publishing Co., Inc.   New York

To Richard—with love and much affection

Embroidery floss on cover courtesy of J. & P. Coats Co.

Library of Congress Cataloging-in-Publication Data

Perna, Sharon.
    Treasury of cross-stitch samplers.

    Includes index.
    1. Cross-stitch—Patterns.   2. Samplers.
I. Title.
TT778.C76P44 1987   746.3   86-23146
ISBN 0-8069-6474-X

              1   3   5   7   9   10   8   6   4   2

Copyright © 1987 by Sharon Perna
Published by Sterling Publishing Co., Inc.
Two Park Avenue, New York, N.Y. 10016
Distributed in Canada by Oak Tree Press Ltd.
c/o Canadian Manda Group, P.O. Box 920, Station U
Toronto, Ontario, Canada M8Z 5P9
Distributed in the United Kingdom by Blandford Press
Link House, West Street, Poole, Dorset BH15 1LL, England
Distributed in Australia by Capricorn Ltd.
P.O. Box 665, Lane Cove, NSW 2066
Manufactured in the United States of America

Contents

Introduction

I have enthusiastically and joyously created 29 cross-stitch samplers of my own design. Now I want to share each of them with you. You have seen samplers and know what they are—those flat pieces of embroidered cloth that are enriched with a variety of motifs and letters. The concept of embroidering a sampler is very old (it first came into use during the sixteenth-century). As I worked with just two simple stitches, the cross-stitch and the backstitch, I found that an enormous wealth of designs can be produced.

Whether or not you have done any needlework lately, or you are just looking for a new project, try making a sampler using these stitches. Cross-stitch is so simple and easy to do, and the flavor of this folk art, which uniquely combines letters, numerals, and pictures, is so appealing. Often the maker's name and date are incorporated into the design, and this gives the picture a charming personal nuance. Since samplers are usually made for the embroiderer's home, for relatives, and friends, the creations are truly an individual and intimate art.

My samplers are divided into two types: Some are family records that document and acquaint you with the names, births, marriages, deaths, and milestones of family members; others are alphabet/verse types that blend letters of the alphabet, numerals, and sayings with a mixture of religious and secular motifs. As you work with each sampler in this book, you will find a list of materials, a cross-stitch color key, instructions, and a charted graph. The charted graph shows exactly where each color and stitch should be placed on the sampler. Mounting and framing suggestions are also provided. Most important of all, however, is the fact that throughout the text, I have tried to share my expertise, successes, and even the knowledge gained from failures so that your sewing experience will be delightful, attractive, and rewarding.

I know you will enjoy making samplers because they require so few supplies: You only need evenweave cloth, cotton embroidery floss (thread), needles, and scissors. With so little equipment required, it is plain to see why cross-stitch projects are also easy to transport, set up, and pick up to work on for a few minutes or hours. Have I convinced you to give one a try? Samplers are so much fun to embroider, and best of all, they speak to us with hearts and hands.

Happy stitching!

METRIC EQUIVALENCY CHART

MM—MILLIMETRES   CM—CENTIMETRES

INCHES TO MILLIMETRES AND CENTIMETRES

Inches	MM	CM	Inches	CM	Inches	CM
⅛	3	0.3	9	22.9	30	76.2
¼	6	0.6	10	25.4	31	78.7
⅜	10	1.0	11	27.9	32	81.3
½	13	1.3	12	30.5	33	83.8
⅝	16	1.6	13	33.0	34	86.4
¾	19	1.9	14	35.6	35	88.9
⅞	22	2.2	15	38.1	36	91.4
1	25	2.5	16	40.6	37	94.0
1¼	32	3.2	17	43.2	38	96.5
1½	38	3.8	18	45.7	39	99.1
1¾	44	4.4	19	48.3	40	101.6
2	51	5.1	20	50.8	41	104.1
2½	64	6.4	21	53.3	42	106.7
3	76	7.6	22	55.9	43	109.2
3½	89	8.9	23	58.4	44	111.8
4	102	10.2	24	61.0	45	114.3
4½	114	11.4	25	63.5	46	116.8
5	127	12.7	26	66.0	47	119.4
6	152	15.2	27	68.6	48	121.9
7	178	17.8	28	71.1	49	124.5
8	203	20.3	29	73.7	50	127.0

YARDS TO METRES

Yards	Metres	Yards	Metres	Yards	Metres	Yards	Metres	Yards	Metres
⅛	0.11	2⅛	1.94	4⅛	3.77	6⅛	5.60	8⅛	7.43
¼	0.23	2¼	2.06	4¼	3.89	6¼	5.72	8¼	7.54
⅜	0.34	2⅜	2.17	4⅜	4.00	6⅜	5.83	8⅜	7.66
½	0.46	2½	2.29	4½	4.11	6½	5.94	8½	7.77
⅝	0.57	2⅝	2.40	4⅝	4.23	6⅝	6.06	8⅝	7.89
¾	0.69	2¾	2.51	4¾	4.34	6¾	6.17	8¾	8.00
⅞	0.80	2⅞	2.63	4⅞	4.46	6⅞	6.29	8⅞	8.12
1	0.91	3	2.74	5	4.57	7	6.40	9	8.23
1⅛	1.03	3⅛	2.86	5⅛	4.69	7⅛	6.52	9⅛	8.34
1¼	1.14	3¼	2.97	5¼	4.80	7¼	6.63	9¼	8.46
1⅜	1.26	3⅜	3.09	5⅜	4.91	7⅜	6.74	9⅜	8.57
1½	1.37	3½	3.20	5½	5.03	7½	6.86	9½	8.69
1⅝	1.49	3⅝	3.31	5⅝	5.14	7⅝	6.97	9⅝	8.80
1¾	1.60	3¾	3.43	5¾	5.26	7¾	7.09	9¾	8.92
1⅞	1.71	3⅞	3.54	5⅞	5.37	7⅞	7.20	9⅞	9.03
2	1.83	4	3.66	6	5.49	8	7.32	10	9.14

Materials and Techniques

Materials

AIDA CLOTH

My samplers are worked on a popular evenweave fabric called aida cloth. "Evenweave" means that the fabric has the same number of threads to the inch in both directions, the warp (lengthwise) and filling or woof (crosswise) threads. The evenweave you will use for your sampler has a woven grid made by the crossing of the threads; the charted graph you will work from also has a corresponding grid for you to follow.

Aida cloth is a 100 percent cotton fabric that can be purchased in needlecraft, fabric, craft, and many department stores. It is available in white, ivory, and a variety of colors. Sold in precut pieces with measurements that differ from one manufacturer to another (12" x 18", 18" x 20", 18" x 40", 36" x 36", or 36" x 60"), aida cloth is also available in bolts of 40", 42", 43", 51", and 60" widths that can be cut to your exact needs. This cloth is also woven with a specific number of threads per inch. Called the thread count, aida comes in counts of 8, 11, 14, and 18. When a particular design calls for a certain count and the instructions are ignored, the final size of the embroidery will be altered and distorted. In all of these samplers, aida cloth with a count of 11 is required.

There are four things to learn about aida cloth: The cloth is never laundered before you do the embroidery; the cloth frays easily; the cloth shrinks up naturally in areas where there is a heavy concentration of cross-stitching; and the fabric shrinks anywhere from 1/2" to 3/4" after the finished item is washed with soap and water. None of the above characteristics are bad. In fact, shrinking and tighten-ing after washing it gives the finished product a nice, neat look. As for the fraying, you can avoid it by using one of the following methods: Turn under 1/4" on the raw edges of the aida cloth; press this towards the wrong side of the fabric. Then finish off the raw edges by either of these methods: Whip around the edges, using a knotted, double strand of matching thread (Illus. 1); machine-stitch with straight stitching twice, 1/8" from the edges (Illus. 2); or machine-

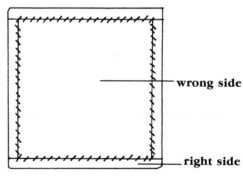

Illus. 1. To avoid fraying, use a whipping stitch on the cut edges of the aida cloth.

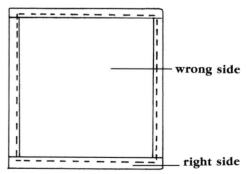

Illus. 2. Machine-stitch around the edges before you begin embroidering.

stitch with zigzag stitching twice around the piece (Illus. 3).

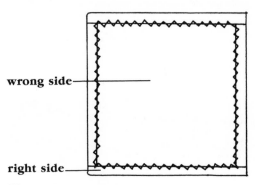

Illus. 3. Zigzag stitching on your machine prevents fraying.

SIX-STRAND EMBROIDERY FLOSS

Six-strand cotton embroidery floss is available in a wide range of brilliant colors. (The word "floss" has increasingly been used by thread companies to describe six-strand cotton embroidery thread. Therefore, the words "floss" and "thread" have become interchangeable in embroidery terminology when referring to six-strand embroidery cotton.) Marketed in inexpensive skeins, each skein includes approximately 9 yards. The thread can be used with all 6 strands or divided into smaller groups from 1 to 5 strands. For the samplers in this book 2 strands of floss, cut into 12" to 14" lengths, are ideal for the cross-stitching and backstitching required on 11-count aida cloth.

Embroidery floss is strong, delicate in appearance, and washable. Thread that is washable can be a plus or minus. For example, in the DMC floss (mouliné spécial), I have had experiences where the reds, oranges, and dark blues (the colors made with naphthol dyes) have bled. So I always advise that these particular colors should be tested for colorfastness before they are used. To test them, wash the floss in plenty of lukewarm water. If the color runs, continue rinsing with sufficient amounts of cold water until the bleeding stops. Remove the floss from the sink without wringing and place on a towel. Press off the excess moisture with the towel, and let the floss dry. Then start embroidering.

The J. & P. Coats floss that I use is usually colorfast. I have found, however, that if a sampler with lots of red is washed by hand and the weather is so humid that the piece takes more than a day to dry, the colors might bleed. If this happens to your sampler, rewash it in a washing machine, and dry it in a clothesdryer. Often the excess dye will completely wash out or, at least, fade considerably.

NO. 24 TAPESTRY NEEDLES

Tapestry needles are sold individually or in packages. They vary in size from no. 13 (the heaviest) to no. 26 (the finest). For the 11-count aida cloth used in these samplers, a no. 24 needle is the size that you need. Do not use crewel needles, which are intended for embroidery techniques that pierce the threads of the fabric.

Tapestry needles have two characteristics: blunt points and large eyes. The blunt point keeps you from splitting previous stitches, and it allows the needle to slip easily through the holes of the evenweave. The large eye makes threading simpler and keeps the floss from fraying. In short, when the appropriate tools (the right size needle and the proper cloth count) are used, you are on your way to producing beautiful needlework.

THE EXTRAS

Although embroidery fabric, floss, and needles are the basic tools for cross-stitching, you'll also need the following supplies:

Scissors (large and small)
Thimble
Rulers
Use 6", 12" (transparent), and 24" rulers.
Pencils
Graph paper
You'll need graph paper to work out the names, dates, and information that changes on certain samplers. You can buy graph paper in pads or individual sheets at office supply, needlecraft, some variety and stationery shops.

The paper I use is erasable with a grid of 8 squares x 8 squares to the inch. For easy visibility when working, avoid graph paper that has more than 10 or 12 squares to the inch.

Embroidery hoops
Hoops are not necessary and may actually slow down the embroidery. If you feel helpless without one, however, use an adjustable tambour frame (the type with a screw on the outer ring) made of wood or plastic.

Embroidery Stitch Techniques

CROSS-STITCH

Cross-stitches are worked by passing a blunt tapestry needle through the holes of the evenweave. A completed cross-stitch is made in two movements: A bottom stitch, which slants like this /, and a top stitch, which slants like this \. Cross-stitches can be made singly (Illus. 4), or in rows by making the first journey in one direction to form the lower half (Illus. 5) and the return journey in the opposite direction (Illus. 5 and 6). Cross stitches can also be made in horizontal, vertical, and diagonal directions. The rule of paramount importance: All the stitches must be crossed *in the same direction.*

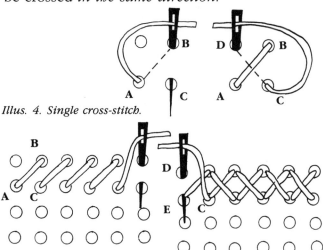

Illus. 4. Single cross-stitch.

Illus. 5. First direction of cross-stitch in rows.
Illus. 6. Return journey of cross-stitch.

BACKSTITCH

Backstitches add detailing to a surface that is predominantly embroidered with cross-stitches. Since they are used as accents, backstitches are done after the cross-stitching is completed. To make a backstitch, bring the needle up through the hole in the evenweave fabric at A. Take a small running stitch backwards to B. Bring the needle up in front of the first stitch at C. Pull the thread through (Illus. 7). Repeat. Like cross-stitches, backstitches can be sewn in several different directions—horizontally, vertically, diagonally, or in combinations (Illus. 8). On the graphs in this book, backstitches are indicated by bold lines; and they are drawn on the charts in the direction they are to be embroidered.

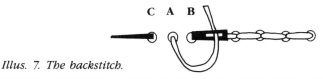

Illus. 7. The backstitch.

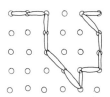

Illus. 8. The backstitch worked in different directions.

EMBROIDERING

To begin your embroidery, cut the six-strand floss into 12" or 14" lengths. Separate each thread color you are using into 2 strands. When you thread the needle, do not make knots at either the beginning or end of the thread. To fasten the end, leave a 1" tail of the thread on the back of the sampler. Make your first cross-stitches as you simultaneously secure the tail by working over it with the next few stitches.

To begin a new thread after you have already worked several rows of embroidery, run your needle under 4 or 5 previously worked stitches on the reverse side of the evenweave. Come up on the right side of the fabric, and cross-stitch as usual.

ENDING A THREAD

To end the thread, run your needle under 4 or 5 stitches on the back of the design. Clip off the excess floss. Remember that the back of the cloth should appear as neat as the front.

FINDING THE STARTING POINT OF THE FIRST CROSS-STITCH

In my samplers, the first stitch is always located in the top left corner of the aida cloth. All samplers are constructed with 3" seam allowances. In the instructions for each piece, specific directions are given for locating the starting point. For example, in "Don't Count Your Chickens," the instructions say, "Measure across 3 1/2" from top left corner; measure downwards 3" from top left corner. Mark point where two measurements intersect" (Illus. 9).

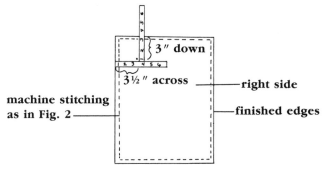

Illus. 9. To locate the starting point of the first cross-stitch, measure from the top left corner of the evenweave.

This spot, temporarily marked by a straight pin, is the starting point for the first cross-stitch. Select the proper color of floss from the cross-stitch color key. Continue by making all the cross-stitches to the right. Complete each row below by working in sequence from left to right and from top to bottom.

READING CHARTED GRAPHS

To reproduce each of the samplers, you will work from a charted graph. In reading the graph, remember that one square on paper represents one square on cloth that will be filled with a complete cross-stitch. The different symbols on the chart represent cross-stitches to be made using particular colors of embroidery floss by either J. & P. Coats or DMC. Backstitches are indicated by a bold line, and they are drawn in the direction they are to be embroidered. Plain squares are areas of the aida cloth that contain no embroidery.

To keep your place on the chart, try either of the following methods: Place an index card or small ruler under the row you are presently working on; or cross out the completed rows with a light-colored pencil or magic marker.

PLANNING LETTERS AND NUMBERS

On all the projects in Family Records and on several of the Verse Samplers, you will be inserting different names, dates, and information in specified sections of the sampler. Since letters and numerals take time to embroider and errors take time to rip out, you must plan and lay out all the information you will use on graph paper before picking up your needle and cloth.

To begin, refer to the project's instructions and the charted graph. First, answer these questions:
1. Which letters and/or numbers are to be used?
2. How many cross-stitches in width are there to work with on each line?
3. How many spaces are allowed between each individual letter within a word or between each individual number within a date?
4. How many spaces are allowed between each complete word and/or date?
5. Are commas and periods needed? How many spaces are required between a word and a comma or a date and punctuation? Is punctuation to be included in the counting?
6. Are the lines centered or lined up the same distance from the margin?

Now, get out your graph paper, ruler, and pencil! If, for example, you are working on the birth column in "Family Register," and you know there are

45 spaces (in width) to fit the date December 22, 1939, it can be done like this: Mark the beginning and end (the width) of the available spaces; then pencil in the lines indicating the height (main body) of the letters and/or numbers and, if needed on some samplers, the lines marking the top of the ascenders (on b, d, f, h, k, and l) and the bottom of the descenders (on g, j, p, q, and y). Within this rectangle, mark an X in each part of the information needed for that line (Illus. 10). If necessary, repeat

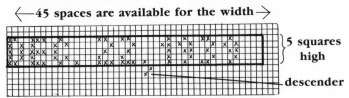

Illus. 10. *Plan and lay out the letters and numbers you will use on graph paper.*

this process for each additional line. (Each X represents a cross-stitch.)

If the lettering goes beyond the available space, something must be eliminated:

Names: Middle names can be reduced to an initial, followed by a period; or you can eliminate middle and family names, allowing the given names to stand alone without the accompaniment of middle or last names. If "and" is needed as a conjunction between names, reduce it to an ampersand (&).

Months: Try condensing the entire word to the first 3 letters, followed by a period; for example, use Jan., Feb., Mar., Apr., Jun., Jul., Aug., Sep., Oct., Nov., and Dec.

Dates of the same century: Consider abbreviating them, for instance, as '46 and '84 instead of 1946 and 1984.

As for long *states:* Try substituting the old or new postal abbreviations, such as Okla. or OK for Oklahoma, Miss. or MS for Mississippi.

If the planned lettering fills only a small portion, and the sampler seems bare, add more information. For short names, consider adding the middle or last name. If the project calls for just a state, as in "In Loving Memory," add the city as well. Or if your college or university has a very brief name, as in "Graduation," add college or university following the name. Extending a line is usually not a dilemma; having too little space is the typical situation.

When you know what information is to be included and have planned the correct spacing, refer to your charted graph as your new stitch guide. Check lastly, however, to see if all the information needs to be lined up against one margin or if the line is centered.

Finishing Techniques

WASHING

The finished sampler needs to be hand- or machine-washed before mounting and framing it. To do this, use lukewarm water and Ivory soap. Wash and rinse thoroughly. If you plan to drip-dry the sampler, place it while still wet in a colorfast terry towel. Then roll and pat it to absorb the excess moisture. Hang the sampler so that it is smooth and wrinkle-free. For machine-drying, remove the sampler while it is still slightly damp.

IRONING

Press the sampler several times on the wrong side of the fabric, using a setting of COTTON and STEAM. Then lay the article flat until all the dampness has completely evaporated.

MOUNTING

After the sampler is washed, pressed, and thoroughly dried, it will be ready to mount on a panel. The panel is a combination of mat board, polyester batting, and unbleached muslin. To mount each sampler I recommend the following materials and directions.

Materials needed:

    3 pieces of white *mat board* (Try to use acid-free 100 percent rag board, also called museum board.)

    1 sheet of Polyfil traditional *batting* (100 percent polyester)

    1 piece of washed *unbleached muslin* (white or ivory)

    1'' *masking tape*

    3 or 4 skeins of white or ivory *six-strand embroidery floss*

    Any bright color of regular *sewing thread*

    6'' and 24'' *rulers*

    Mat knife

    Pliers

    A large *crewel needle*

    Straight pins

Directions:

1. In the instructions for each sampler, I suggest that you add a specified 3/4'' to 1 1/2'' margin on all four sides of the design before you begin mounting the sampler. This additional dimension, which intrudes into the 3'' seam allowances planned for each sampler, provides a breather between the edge of the actual embroidery and the edge of the custom frame. For example, to mark off a 3/4'' margin on "Roots and Wings," use this procedure:

■ On one side of the sampler, locate the very edge of the embroidery.

■ Measure 3/4'' beyond this point (Illus. 11), and temporarily mark the spot with a straight pin.

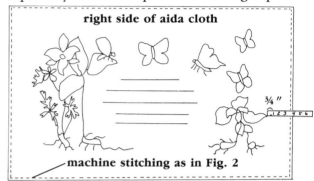

Illus. 11. To add a specified 3/4" margin to all sides of the design, measure from the very edge of the embroidery.

■ Count how many squares on the aida cloth there are between the pin and measurement (probably about 9 squares).

■ On the three remaining sides of the sampler, mark off the 3/4'' (the 9 or whatever squares) from the very edge of the embroidery.

■ With a knotted, single strand of the bright-colored sewing thread, connect these four points by sewing straight lines. Weave in and out of the aida cloth with long basting stitches (Illus. 12). These threaded lines will now indicate the edge of the mounted sampler.

Illus. 12. With the 3/4" margin added, the basting stitches now indicate the actual edge of the sampler.

2. In two or three places, take the length and width measurements of this new shape and write them on your chart. These new dimensions will be the finished size of your sampler.

3. Cut 3 pieces of mat board, each measuring the dimensions in step 2. Stack them together; tape once in middle of each side.

4. Cut 1 sheet of polyester batting the same size as 1 mat board. Lay the batting on top. Tape all four layers once in the middle of each side (Illus. 13).

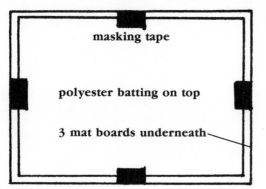

Illus. 13. View of front when batting is taped on mat boards.

5. Cut 1 piece of washed unbleached muslin. To get this measurement, add a 2" seam allowance to the dimensions in step 2. With right sides up, place the middle of the muslin over the approximate midpoint of the batting-mat board pile. On the reverse side of the pile, fold in the top and bottom; tape temporarily. Fold in the sides of the muslin; tape. Get the corners of the muslin neat and flat; tape temporarily (Illus. 14.)

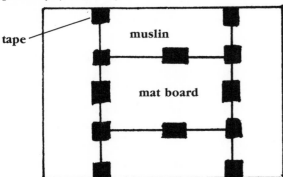

Illus. 14. View of back when taping.

6. With right side down, lay the sampler flat; lay the muslin-batting-mat board combination over the sampler and within the finished edge of the design lines. Fold in the top and bottom of the sampler; tape temporarily to the back of the mat board. If necessary, tightly pull the fabric to get the edge of the design lines on the edge of the mat board. Fold in the sides; get the edge of the design lines on the edge of the mat board; tape. Get the corners neat and flat by either taping or pinning them.

7. On the back of the sampler, sew the four corners flat with 1/2" running stitches. Use a crewel needle and all 6 strands of embroidery floss. If necessary, use the pliers to pull the needle through. Remove the tape and pins in this area.

8. On the back of the sampler, lace back and forth between the top and bottom edges of the cloth. Use the knotted 6 strands of floss, cut in 1 1/2-yard lengths. To lace, start at one side of the sampler and work towards the opposite end. Insert the needle 1/8" beyond the folded and stitched edges of the aida; and lace back and forth. As you approach the end of each thread, check to see that the edge of the design line rests on the edge of the mat board. If it does not, tighten up the lacing. Check also to see that the front of the sampler is centered, flat, and slightly taut. Remove any tape that remains on this side (Illus. 15).

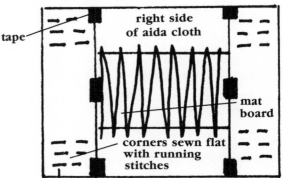

Illus. 15. View of back and lacing in first direction.

9. Lace in the opposite direction by starting at one end and moving across to the other. Check to see that the edge of the design is on the edge of the mat board. Remove any remaining tape (Illus. 16).

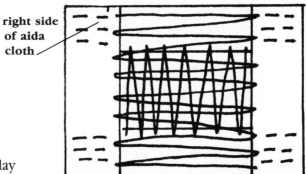

Illus. 16. View of back and lacing in second direction.

10. Pull out the bastings on the edge of the design. Add a custom frame.

FRAMING

Framing insures a safe and proper support for permanent display of the mounted sampler. In formal framing, mats, glass, or Plexiglas acrylic plastic are usually added. If you can resist, it is better to prevent the textile from coming in contact with paper, plastic, or glass. As I am interested in fabric conservation, my advice is to just add a frame, and let the fabric breathe.

Helpful Hints

THE DO'S

■ Use guidelines. In certain areas of the sampler that will carry names (Illus. 17), dates, and borders (Illus. 18) that are undulating (the edge of the design moves in a wavy line), guidelines are very helpful.

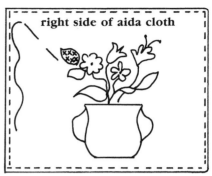

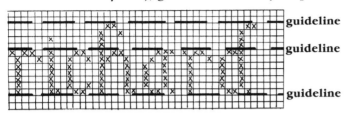

guideline
guideline
guideline

Illus. 17. Right side of aida cloth with cross-stitches and guidelines.

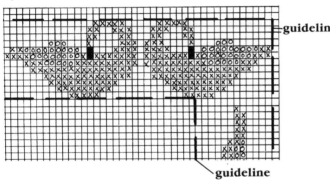

guideline

guideline

Illus. 18. Right side of aida cloth with three colors of cross-stitches (indicated by the X's, O's, and solid squares) and guidelines.

Basically, guidelines are temporary straight lines (basting stitches) that are formed by weaving a knotted, single-strand of bright-colored thread in and out of the holes in the aida evenweave. Add them as you start embroidering a tricky section of the design; when your cross-stitching is completely finished, remove the guidelines. When used properly, these guidelines are time-savers because they keep counting confined to a smaller area of the fabric. As you work within this defined section, if a stitch happens to go beyond the basted territory, you will quickly notice the error and correct it. (The stitch shouts out as a voice in the wilderness!)

■ Carry your embroidery floss to a new area, if the thread can be run under previous stitches. For example, if you are using dark hunter's green on one leaf in the top of a bouquet and the color appears again on a lower stem, do not end the color in the first position. Instead, carry the floss to an out-of-the-way spot on the sampler. Come up on the right side of the fabric, and let the floss dangle until it is needed (Illus. 19). At that time, rethread the needle with the reserved floss and travel on the wrong

Illus. 19. Letting the thread dangle until it is ready to be used again.

side of the cloth to the new location by going under previously embroidered stitches. Then continue your embroidering as usual.

THE DON'TS

■ Don't preshrink aida cloth.

■ Don't carry the floss for more than 5 squares across the back of an open area of aida (loose and dark threads will show through the front of the fabric).

■ Don't leave your needle or embroidery hoop on the fabric when you are not embroidering (both leave rust marks).

■ Don't bleed on your sampler. This may sound silly, but blood is one of the most difficult stains to remove from light-colored textiles. If you prick your finger and bleed, staining the sampler, immediately wash it out with cold water. If that is not enough, run an old toothbrush over a bar of soap and scrub out the spot.

■ Don't use Scotchgard carpet and upholstery protector on your needlework. This treatment may be fine for upholstery, but I have noticed that the chemical makes embroidery floss color run. Since the Scotchgard product does not let water penetrate the fibres, the mistake cannot be washed away.

■ Don't hang your sampler on walls in direct sunlight. Light causes fading and the breakdown of textile fibres. Severe temperature changes and high humidity also accelerate textile damage.

■ Don't hang your sampler over the mantle of a functioning fireplace; the soot and smoke will ruin it.

■ Don't store your framed sampler in a plastic bag. Instead, wrap it in washed unbleached muslin or in a clean pillowcase, and tilt the standing frame slightly. Store the covered embroidery where there is good air circulation. Try to keep it dry and clean by frequently inspecting it. Attics and basements are usually not the best storage places.

Sampler Recap

This list recapitulates the most important information that you should remember:

1. All of the samplers are made with either white or ivory 11-count aida evenweave.

2. Two strands of cotton floss and a no. 24 tapestry needle are used for all cross-stitching and back-stitching.

3. Don't launder aida cloth before you start to embroider.

4. Follow this basic routine when working on all samplers:

■ Cut your cloth according to instructions for "cut size" (3" seam allowances are included in the measurements). Finish the raw edges on all four sides by either hand- or machine-stitching.

■ Find the starting point for the first cross-stitch in the upper left corner of the fabric.

■ Study the cross-stitch key and graph. One square on paper equals 1 stitch on evenweave. Each key gives symbols representing each particular color. Wherever that symbol appears, make a cross-stitch in the appropriate color of embroidery floss. Backstitches are indicated by a bold line, and they are drawn on the chart in the direction they are to be embroidered. The plain squares represent areas where there is no embroidery.

■ Start embroidering. Do the cross-stitches first; add the backstitches later. Never knot the threads. The back of the sampler should be as neat as the front.

■ Wash the finished embroidery. Partially dry and press. Let it dry thoroughly. The cloth will shrink and tighten.

■ Add the specified margin to all four sides of the sampler. Mount the design on a panel, which is a combination of 3 mat boards, 1 layer of polyester batting, and 1 layer of washed unbleached muslin with a 2" seam allowance.

■ Add a frame. Glass is not necessary. Let the fabric breathe.

Family-Record Samplers

Teddy Bear

(Color page A)

Degree of work: easy
Fabric: white aida (11 count)
Cut size of fabric needed: 19" wide x 17"
Finished size: approximately 14 5/8" x 12"

Cross-Stitch Color Key

Symbol	J. & P. Coats six-strand floss	or DMC six-strand floss
☒	51C Gold Brown	436
◆	1 White	Snow-White
Ⅱ	46A Mid Rose	3326
◩	69 Lt. Steel Blue	809
L	223 Sun Gold	743
3	37 Dk. Lavender	554
■	12 Black	310
Q	215 Apple Green	471
•	81B Dk. Colonial Brown	801
☐	Fabric as is	

Purchase 2 skeins of 51C Gold Brown. Buy 1 skein of each remaining color.

To find the starting point of the first cross-stitch: Measure across 3" from top left corner; measure downwards 3" from top left corner. Mark point where these two measurements intersect. Start embroidering at top left outer corner on gold brown border.

Areas of special concern: Change the child's name, date, and weight lines. Select colors to personalize the sampler for your child. See alphabet no. 7 and numeral no. 6. On the name and birth lines, there are 111 spaces in width available (that leaves

Illus. 20.

a minimum of at least 4 spaces at the beginning and end of line). There are 27 spaces available on the pound and ounce lines; start the numerals in the position shown on the chart and leave at least 3 spaces blank at the end. On second and third lines, words and colons "born:" and "weight:" stay as and where they are. Leave 1 space between each letter, between word and punctuation, between date and comma, and between numerals within a date. Leave 5 spaces between each complete word, between punctuation and words, and between punctuation and dates. Align the name and birth lines an equal number of spaces from the left margin.

Margin to be added when mounting: Add 1" borders on all four sides of the embroidery.

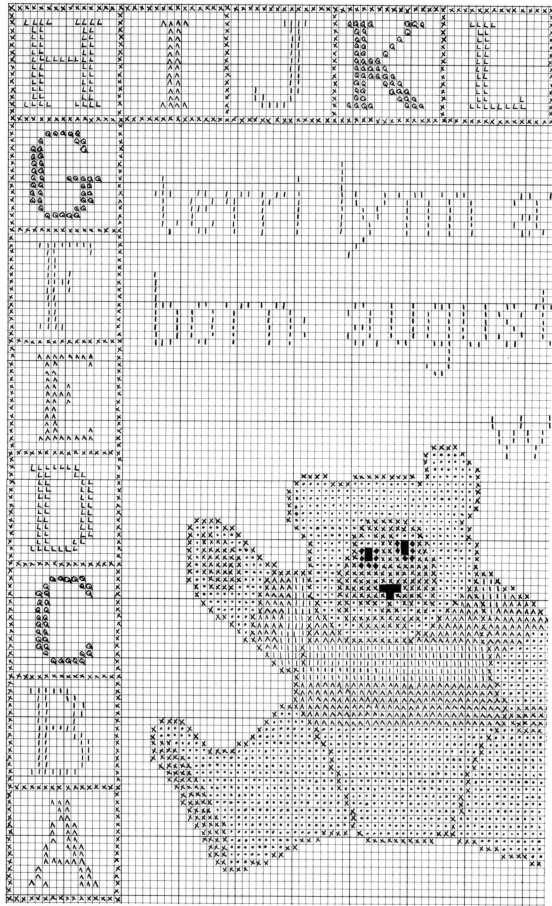

Illus. 21. Charted graph for "Teddy Bear."

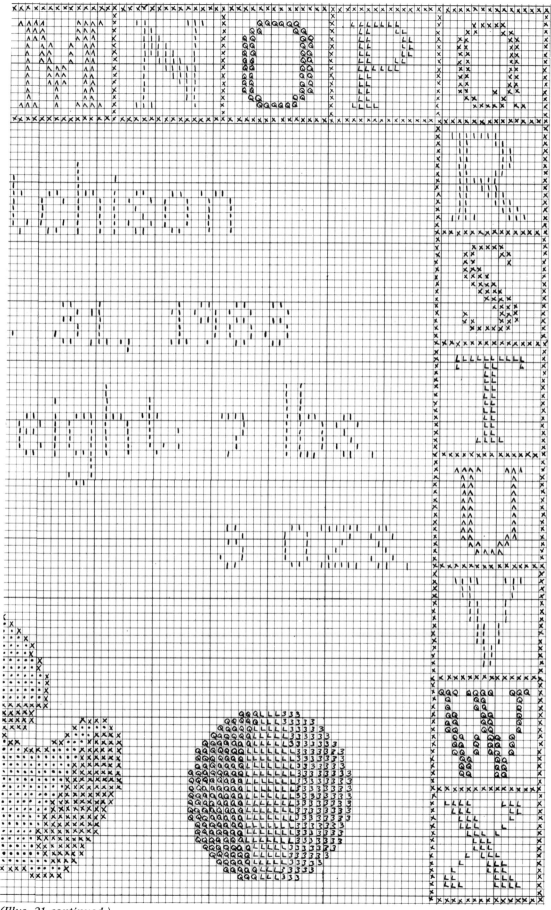

(Illus. 21 continued.)

Degree of work: easy
Fabric: white aida (11 count)
Cut size of fabric needed: 18" wide x 22"
Finished size: approximately 12 1/8" x 16 7/8"

Cross-Stitch Color Key

Symbol	J. & P. Coats six-strand floss	or DMC six-strand floss
◿	223 Sun Gold	743
·	140 Signal Red	321
⊠	44 Royal Blue	824
3	99 Grass Green	703
■	36 Royal Purple	550
◆	38B Tangerine	947
☐	Fabric as is	

Purchase 2 skeins of 140 Signal Red. Buy 1 skein of each remaining color.

To find the starting point of the first cross-stitch: Measure across 4" from top left corner; measure downwards 3" from top left corner. Mark the point where these two measurements intersect. Start embroidering the head of the small yellow duck at the top left corner of the design.

Areas of special concern: Change the name, date, weight, and time lines. See alphabet no. 13 and numerals no. 8. There are 129 spaces in width to work with (exact length of blue cross-stitch lines above and below the data.) "Birth record of" remains in each sampler. Leave 1 space between each letter within a word, between numerals and punctuation, between letters and punctuation, and be-

Illus. 22.

tween numerals within a date. Leave 5 spaces between each complete word and between complete numbers and words (forget the punctuation when counting). Use decorative diamonds to separate the data; leave 2 or 3 spaces between diamonds and words. If the baby's name is very short, all the information may fit in three rather than four lines. Center each line.

Margin to be added when mounting: Add 3/4" borders on all four sides of the embroidery.

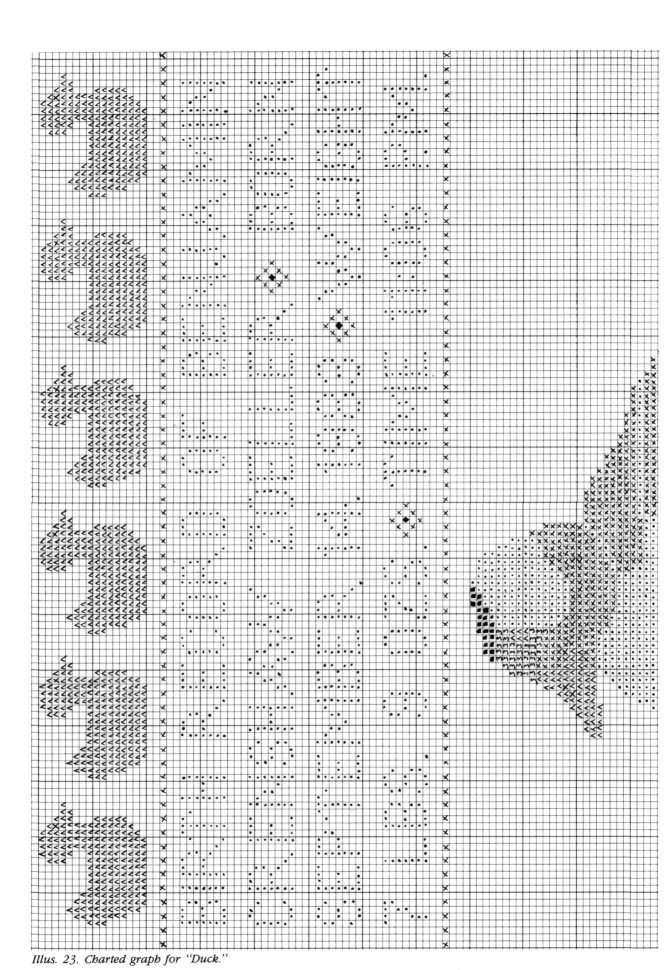

Illus. 23. Charted graph for "Duck."

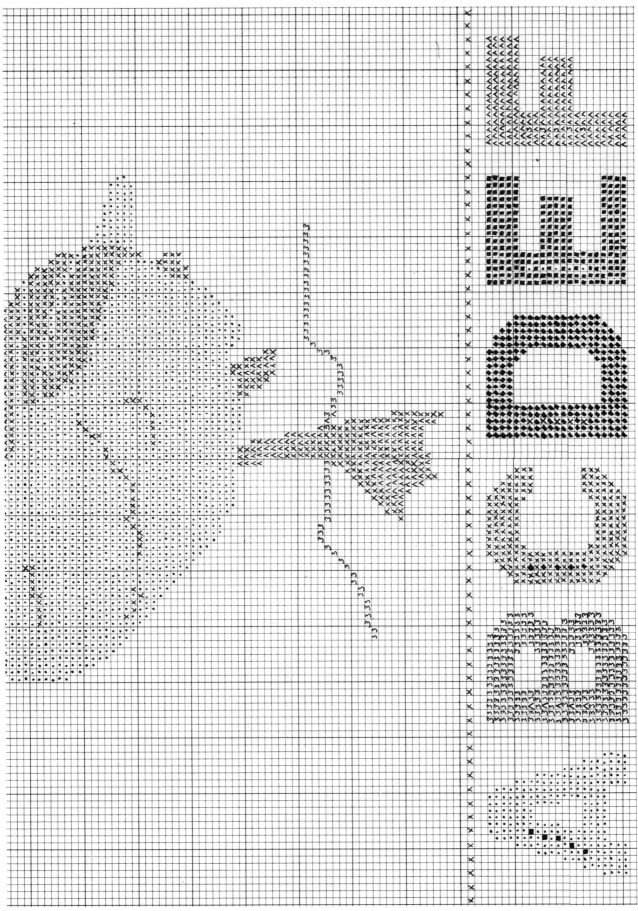

(Illus. 23 continued.)

Happy Birthday

Degree of work: moderate
Fabric: ivory aida (11 count)
Cut size of fabric needed: 21" wide x 18"
Finished size: approximately 16" x 13 1/4"

Cross-Stitch Color Key

Symbol	J. & P. Coats six-strand floss	or DMC six-strand floss
⊠	44 Royal Blue	796
◆	252 Chinese Yellow	307
▬	141 Devil Red	666
·	8 Blue	800
c	245 Atlantic Blue	799
L	46A Mid Rose	3326
◘	122 Watermelon	961
3	81B Dk. Colonial Brown	801
▽	223 Sun Gold	743
◩	132A Parakeet	996
■	5A Chartreuse	704
e	38 Dk. Orange	741
z	28 Myrtle	700
s	4A Mid Pink	818
+	51C Gold Brown	436
Q	69 Lt. Steel Blue	809
☐	Fabric as is	

Backstitch Color Key

Symbol	Color	Code
⊞	44 Royal Blue	796
	141 Devil Red	666
	81B Dk. Colonial Brown	801
	122 Watermelon	961

Purchase 2 skeins of 44 Royal Blue. Buy 1 skein of each remaining color.

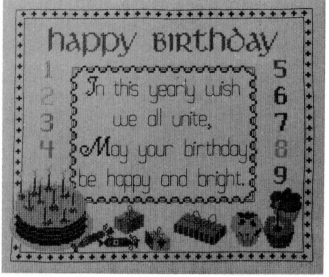

Illus. 24.

To find the starting point of the first cross-stitch: Measure across 3 1/8" from top left corner; measure downwards 3" from top left corner. Mark point where these two measurements intersect. Start embroidering the blue backstitches in the top left corner; then continue with the first blue diamond.

Area of backstitch (indicated by bold lines on charted graph): *44 Royal Blue*—two outer rectangles; birthday verse; wicks on candles; and ribbons on red and turquoise crackers. *141 Devil Red*—two inner rectangles; and ribbons on orange and blue boxes. *81B Dk. Colonial Brown*—ribbon on pink box; and lines on bottom of orange cupcake. *122 Watermelon*—Lines on bottom of yellow and turquoise cupcakes.

Margin to be added when mounting: Add 3/4" borders on all four sides of the embroidery.

Illus. 25. Charted graph for "Happy Birthday."

(Illus. 25 continued.)

Graduation

(Color page B)

Degree of work: moderate
Fabric: ivory aida (11 count)
Cut size of fabric needed: 21" x 21"
Finished size: approximately 16" x 16 3/8"

Cross-Stitch Color Key

Symbol	J. & P. Coats six-strand floss	or DMC six-strand floss
☒	28 Myrtle	700
⊙	99 Grass Green	703
■	1 White	Snow-White
∨	12 Black	310
⊢	90A Bright Gold	783
3	71 Pewter Grey	415
S	81 Dk. Brown	434
Z	51C Gold Brown	436
▲	140 Signal Red	321
⧄	143 Lt. Cardinal	815
☐	Fabric as is	

Backstitch Color Key

⊞	71 Pewter Grey	415
	12 Black	310

Purchase 2 skeins each of 12 Black and 99 Grass Green. Buy 1 skein of each remaining color.

To find the starting point of the first cross-stitch: Measure across 9 3/4" from top left corner; measure downwards 3" from top left corner. Mark the point where these two measures intersect. Start embroidering the first black stitch at top of the arch.

Areas of special concern: Change the name, school and date lines. See alphabet no. 13 and numerals no. 7. There are 110 spaces in width to work with (that leaves a minimum of 2 spaces on

Illus. 26.

either side of the black border). Leave 1 space between each letter within a word and one space between each numeral within a date. Leave 7 spaces between each complete word, between month and day, and between day and year. Position comma 1 space after day, but ignore it in overall counting. The word "the" in line 2 is optional. If dropped, recenter the line. "University" can be shortened to "U." Center each line.

Area of backstitch (indicated by bold lines on charted graph): *71 Pewter Grey*—left edge of diploma. *12 Black*—all other places.

Margin to be added when mounting: Add 13/16" borders on all four sides of the embroidery.

Illus. 27. (Opposite) Charted graph for "Graduation."

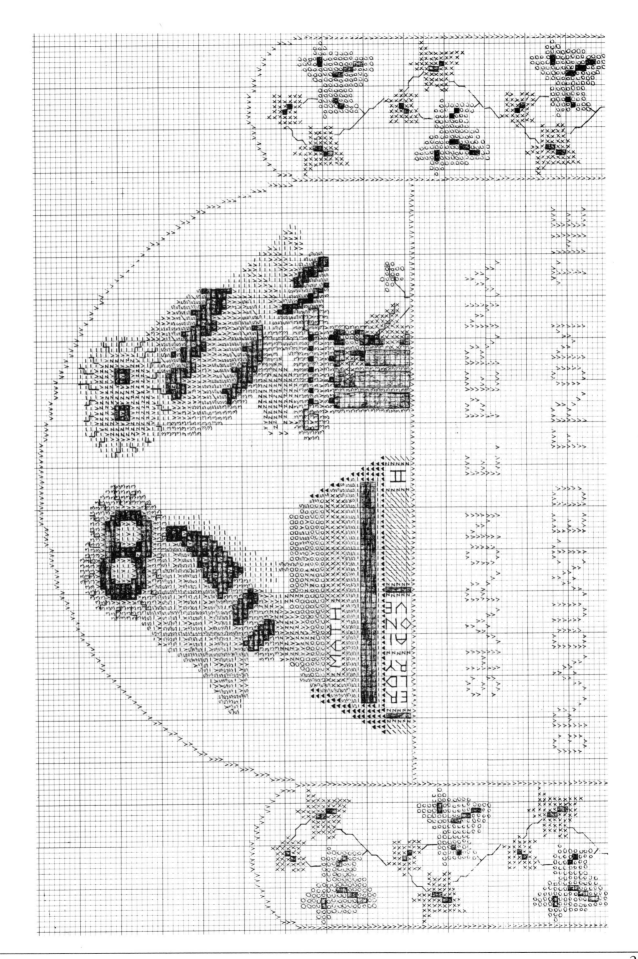

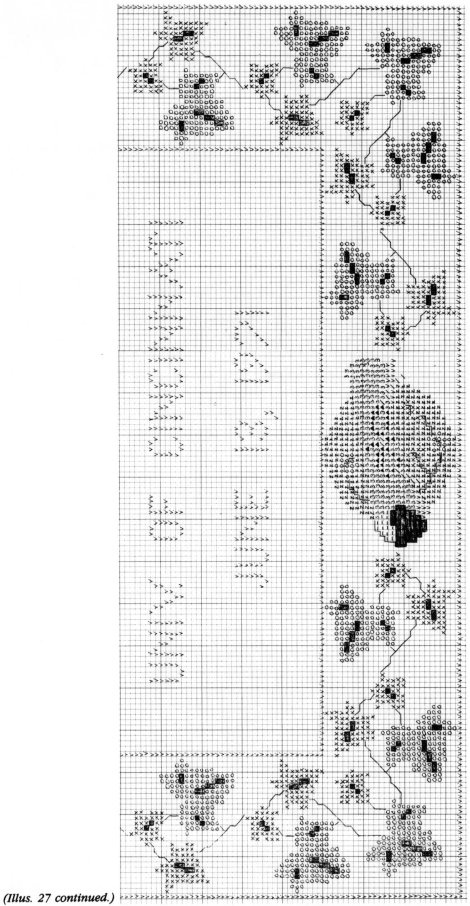

(Illus. 27 continued.)

Cupid

Illus. 28.

Degree of work: easy
Fabric: white aida (11 count)
Cut size of fabric needed: 19" wide x 16"
Finished size: approximately 15" x 11"

Cross-Stitch Color Key

Symbol	J. & P. Coats six-strand floss	or DMC six-strand floss
◱	24A Oriental Blue	518
S	11 Orange	972
▲	62 Russet	435
3	124 Indian Pink	353
X	213 Beige	644
O	46A Mid Rose	3326
·	143 Lt. Cardinal	815
U	Use DMC 775	775
Z	99 Grass Green	703
■	215 Apple Green	471
☐	Fabric as is	

Buy 1 skein of each color.

To find the starting point of the first cross-stitch: Measure across 4 1/4" from top left corner; measure downwards 3" from top left corner. Mark the point where these two measurements intersect. Start embroidering the first beige decorative square in top left corner of the heart border.

Areas of special concern: Change the name and date lines. For the names, see alphabet no. 21. For the date, see alphabet no. 2. For numerals, see numerals no. 3. On name and date lines, there are 80 spaces in width to work with (exact length of decorative hearts on line two). Decorative hearts surrounding the word "and" stay as and where they are. Leave 1 space between each letter within a word, between each number within a date, and between a number and a comma. Leave 4 spaces between month and day and between comma and year. Center each line.

Margin to be added when mounting: Add 7/8" borders on all four sides of the embroidery.

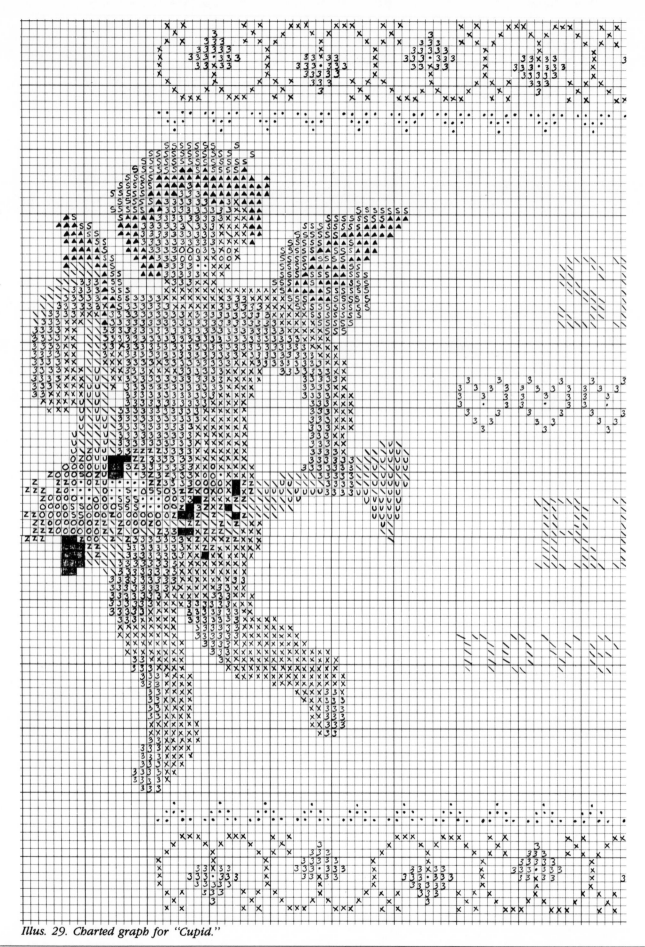

Illus. 29. Charted graph for "Cupid."

(Illus. 29 continued.)

With This Ring I Thee Wed   *(Color page C)*

Degree of work: moderate
Fabric: white aida (11 count)
Cut size of fabric needed: 20" x 20"
Finished size: approximately 15 1/8" wide x 14 1/2"

Illus. 30.

Cross-Stitch Color Key

Symbol	J. & P. Coats six-strand floss	or DMC six-strand floss
·	69 Lt. Steel Blue	809
⊠	223 Sun Gold	743
U	44 Royal Blue	796
■	51C Gold Brown	436
◆	61 Ecru	822
◪	143 Lt. Cardinal	815
L	12 Black	310
△	70 Silver Grey	762
+	1 White	Snow-White
O	211 Charcoal	414
♥	Use DMC 642	642
S	215 Apple Green	471
=	5A Chartreuse	704
◣	28B Treeleaf Green	991
▲	216 Avocado	469
3	99 Grass Green	703
♫	81 Dk. Brown	434
▬	Use DMC 221	221
Z	Use DMC 758	758
☐	Fabric as is	

Backstitch Color Key

 All are black

Purchase 3 skeins of 69 Lt. Steel Blue and 2 skeins of 223 Sun Gold. Buy 1 skein of each remaining color.

To find the starting point of the first cross-stitch: Measure across 3" from top left corner; measure downwards 3" from top left corner. Mark the point where these two measurements intersect. Start embroidering the royal blue triangle in top left corner of design.

Areas of special concern: Change the names, date, and signature lines. For names and signature

line, see alphabet no. 4. For date, see alphabet no. 9. See numerals no. 5. There are 128 spaces in width to work with on name, date, and signature lines (that leaves a minimum of 2 blank spaces at the beginning and end of the line). "With This Ring I Thee Wed" stays as and where it is. Leave 1 space between each letter within a word, between numerals within a date, and between a date and a comma. Leave 3 spaces between complete words, between words and a date, and between comma and a date. To fill in spaces at end of all four lines, use as many repeat motifs as possible. On name and signature lines, leave 1 space between each complete motif. On the date line, leave 2 spaces between each heart and diamond. If, however, the required information is too long, omit these details. Line up all data at an equal distance from the left border.

Area of backstitch (indicated by bold lines on charted graph): all black.

Margin to be added when mounting: Add 1" borders on all four sides of the embroidery.

Illus. 31. Charted graph for "With This Ring I Thee Wed."

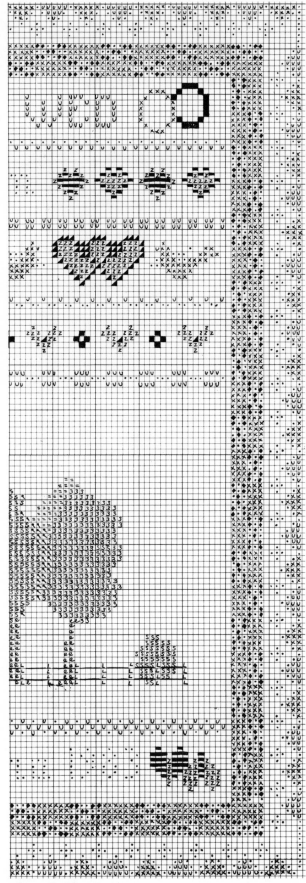

(Illus. 31 continued.)

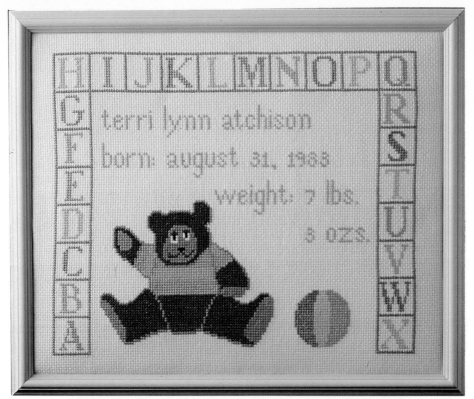

Illus. A1. "Teddy Bear." Birth records make wonderful gifts and heirlooms.

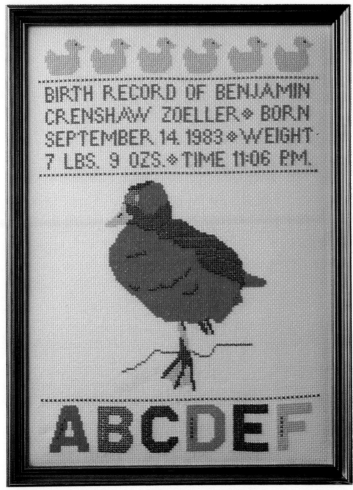

Illus. A2. "Duck." This bright sampler is a variation of the birth record theme.

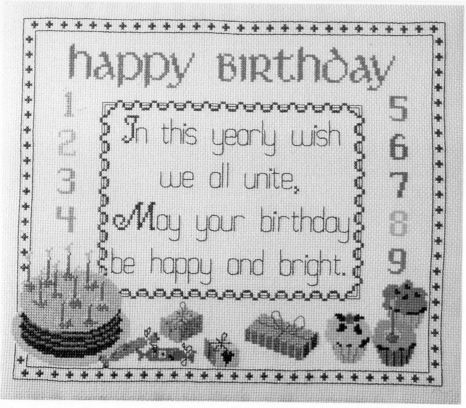

Illus. B1. "Happy Birthday." The anonymous verse in this cheery sampler came from an antique card.

Illus. B2. "Graduation." A sampler is a fabulous and lasting celebration of a graduation.

Illus. C1. "Cupid." For an important couple, what could be nicer than a personal sampler?

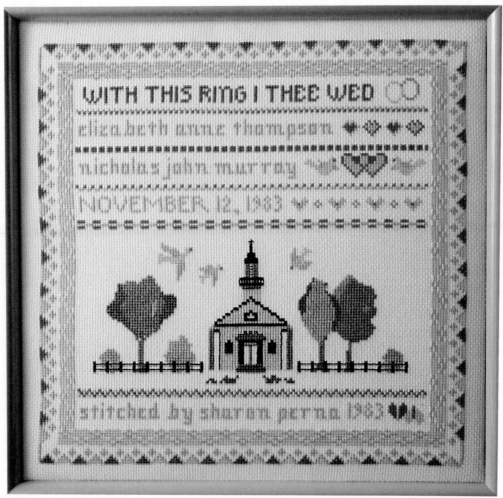

Illus. C2. "With This Ring I Thee Wed." On a day filled with promises and hopes, a wedding sampler is a spectacular gift.

Illus. D1. "Happy Anniversary." Anniversaries are a chance for a couple to remember their shared experiences—their love, the wedding day, the first home, and the gifts sent with best wishes.

Illus. D2. "In Loving Memory." Mourning pictures were once very common. This contemporary version honors the memory of my extraordinary grandfather.

Illus. E1. "Family Register." A family register officially documents the important milestones of your ancestors.

Illus. E2. "Town." The strawberry vine here encircles alphabets, numerals, and the best buildings in town!

Illus. F1. "Chipmunk among the Vegetables." My father's garden (and the chipmunk in it) inspired this project.

Illus. F2. "Watermelons." This sampler could brighten your home with warm thoughts of summer.

Illus. G1. "Flower Basket." The morning glory has to be one of nature's most beautiful creations. Its delicate and clinging qualities are featured in the three-sided border.

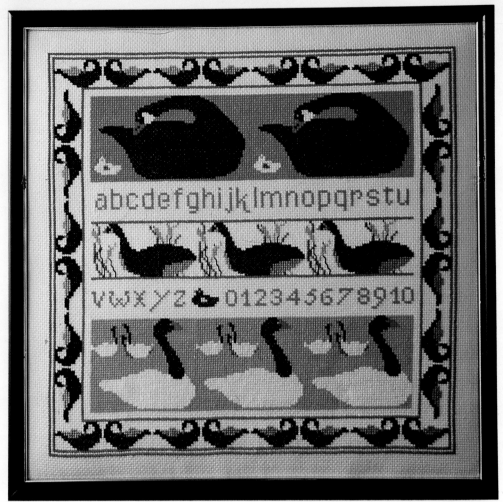

Illus. H1. "Swans." The long, graceful necks and simple shapes of the water bird inspired this sampler.

Illus. H2. "The Early Bird Catches the Worm." This early bird has really caught the juicy worm.

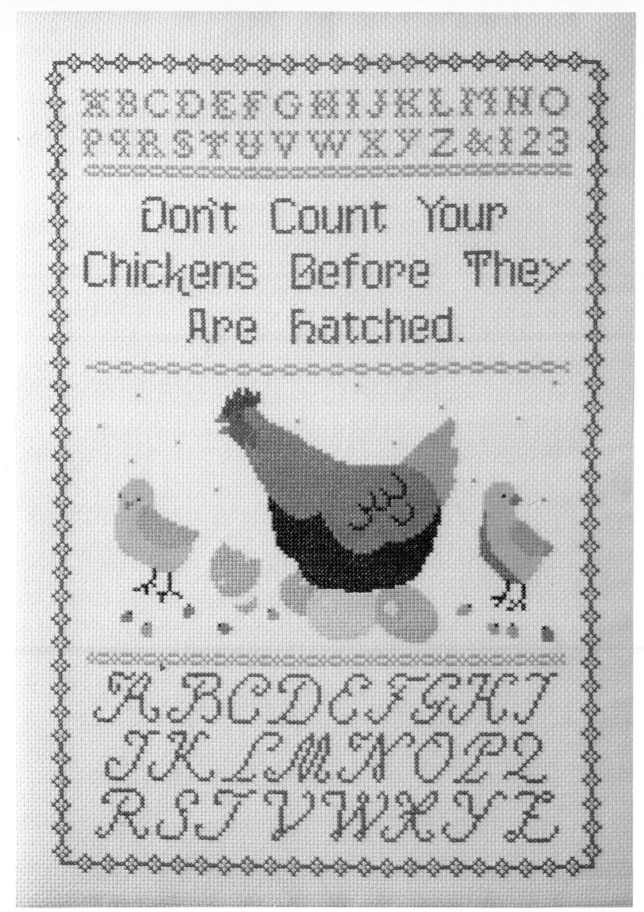

Illus. 11. "Don't Count Your Chickens." The popular English proverb finally became the barnyard inspiration for this work.

Illus. J1. "Home Sweet Home." This saying originally was in the score of the opera "Clari" (premiered in 1823).

Illus. J2. "Bless Our House." The Oakleigh Garden District in Mobile, Alabama, is interesting in this embroidery and in reality.

Illus. K1. "Welcome." The popular pineapple, focal point of this sampler, symbolizes a warm welcome to visitors.

Illus. L1. "Hurray for the Red, White, and Blue." The classic color scheme reinforces this patriotic message.

Illus. L2. "Merry Christmas." With holly, toys, and Santa, this sampler would brighten the holidays.

L

Illus. M1. "Love One Another." Here the warm pink and red palette enhances the love theme from the Bible.

Illus. M2. "God Is Love." The lacelike background contrasts with the pastel flowers and letters.

Illus. N1. "Give Us Our Daily Bread." This phrase from the Lord's Prayer is in Matthew, chapter six.

Illus. N2. "Count Your Blessings." Many people advocate the sentiment of this motto. The numerals strengthen the counting aspect. Different flowers relate the borders to the numerals and words.

Illus. O1. "God, Be Merciful to Me a Sinner." The sinner's prayer is from Luke 18:13.

Illus. O2. "Come, Ye Thankful People." The first verse of the song, "Come, Ye Thankful People, Come," composed in 1844, is featured.

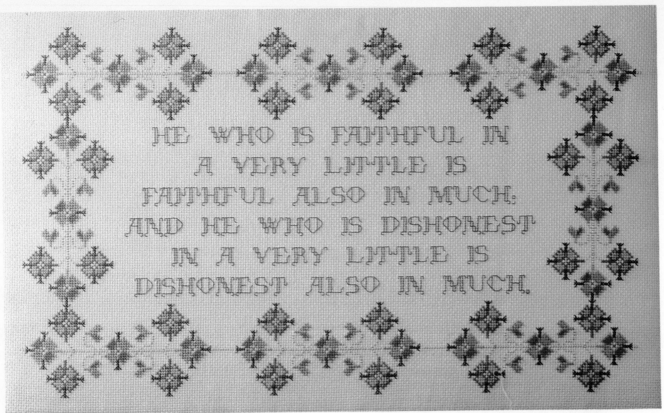

Illus. P1. "He Who Is Faithful." Luke 16:10 is one of my favorite Bible verses.

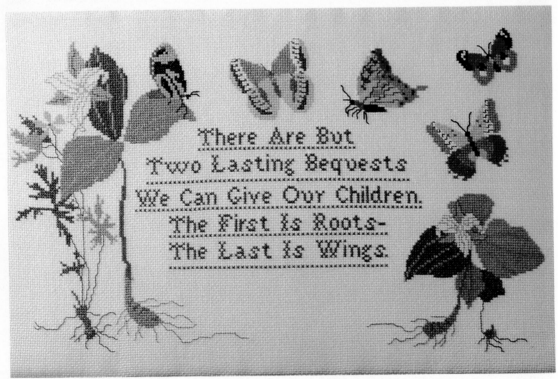

Illus. P2. "Roots and Wings." When I have asked people for their favorite verse, many parents have chosen this simple stanza. In my work, I portrayed examples of roots and wings from nature.

Happy Anniversary

Illus. 32.

Degree of work: challenging
Fabric: white aida (11 count)
Cut size of fabric needed: 25 1/2" wide x 19 1/2"
Finished size: approximately 20 3/4" x 15"

Cross-Stitch Color Key

Symbol	J. & P. Coats six-strand floss	or DMC six-strand floss
☒	12 Black	310
⊡	140 Signal Red	321
⊟	120 Crimson	351
Ⓢ	143 Lt. Cardinal	815
☐	Fabric as is	

Backstitch Color Key

⊞	12 Black	310
	120 Crimson	351
	140 Signal Red	321
	143 Lt. Cardinal	815

Purchase 5 skeins of 12 Black and 4 skeins of 140 Signal Red. Buy 3 skeins of each remaining color.

To find the starting point of the first cross-stitch: Measure across 3" from top left corner; measure downwards 3" from top left edge. Mark the point where these two measurements intersect. Start embroidering the first red heart in top left corner.

Areas of special concern: Change the name and date lines. See alphabet no. 5 and numerals no. 4. There are 149 spaces in width to work with on name and date lines (exact length of "Happy Anniversary"). "Happy Anniversary" stays as and where it is. Leave 1 space between each letter within a word, between each numeral within a date, and between a numeral and a comma. Leave 9 spaces between each full word, between names and double hearts, and between month and day. On the date line, position the year of marriage on left, 3 spaces from the black border; position the year of anniversary on right so that the last numeral is 3 spaces from the black border. If both names are very long, omit hearts at either end. Center each line.

Area of backstitch (indicated by bold lines on charted graph): "With Love" block: *12 Black*—all stems; *120 Crimson*—veins on smallest and largest leaves; *140 Signal Red*—veins on long thin leaves. Bride and groom block: *143 Lt. Cardinal*—ribbons on bouquet; *12 Black*—all other lines. Bell block: *143 Lt. Cardinal*—bell clappers. House block: *140 Signal Red*—all birds; *12 Black*—all other lines. Gift block: *12 Black*—all ribbons. Cooking utensils block: *12 Black*—all lines. Small heart block: *12 Black*—all lines. Heart and rose block: *120 Crimson*—all veins.

Margin to be added when mounting: Add 1" borders on all four sides of the embroidery.

Illus. 33. Charted graph for "Happy Anniversary."

(Illus. 33 continued.)

In Loving Memory

Illus. 34.

Degree of work: moderate
Fabric: white aida (11 count)
Cut size of fabric needed: 24 1/2" wide x 14 1/2"
Finished size: approximately 19 7/8" x 9 7/8"

Cross-Stitch Color Key

Symbol	J. & P. Coats six-strand floss	or DMC six-strand floss
☒	36 Royal Purple	550
⊡	37 Dk. Lavender	554
③	54 Violet	553
⊙	210 Leaf Green	368
⊟	9 Yellow	745
■	26 Nile Green	966
⑤	216 Avocado	469
▽	98 Fern Green	989
☐	Fabric as is	

Backstitch Color Key

⊞	75A Tropic Orange	920

Purchase 2 skeins of 36 Royal Purple. Buy 1 skein of each remaining color.

To find the starting point of the first cross-stitch: Measure across 3" from top left corner; measure downwards 3" from top left corner. Mark the point where these two measurements intersect. Start embroidering the first row at top of light green leaf in the left corner.

Areas of spcial concern: Change the name, birth, and death lines. See alphabet no. 12 and numerals no. 8. There are 156 spaces in width to work with (exact length of birth line). "In Loving" and "Memory Of" lines stay as and where they are. Leave 1 space between each letter within a word. Leave 2 spaces between each number within a date. Leave 7 spaces between each full word and between words and dates with one exception: After both birth and death years, leave 3 spaces, make a decorative diamond, leave 3 spaces before beginning of the state. Center each line.

Area of backstitch (indicated by bold lines on charted graphs): *75A Tropic Orange*—all veins and stems on the clover.

Margin to be added when mounting: Add 1" borders on all four sides of the embroidery.

Illus. 35. Charted graph for "In Loving Memory."

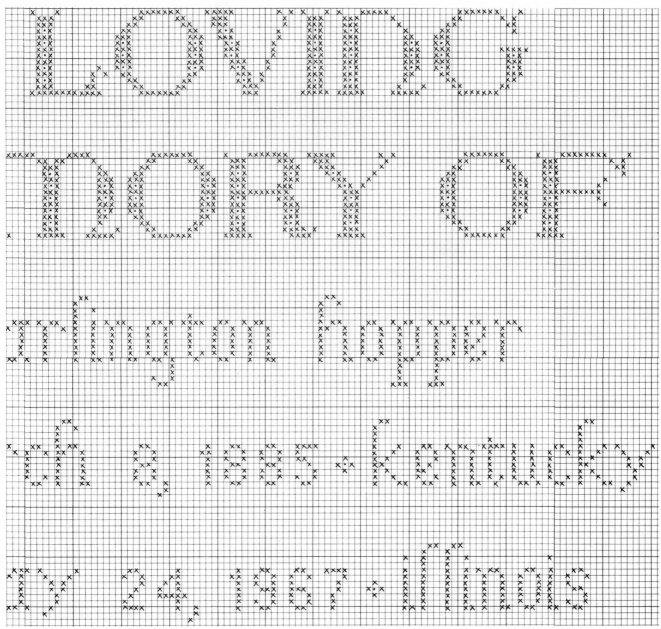

(Illus. 35 continued.)

Family Register

Degree of work: challenging
Fabric: white aida (11 count)
Cut size of fabric needed: 32" wide x 20"
Finished size: approximately 27 1/2" x 15"

Illus. 36.

Cross-Stitch Color Key

Symbol	J. & P. Coats six-strand floss	or DMC six-strand floss
☒	Use DMC 642	642
·	120 Crimson	351
◿	62 Russet	435
⊟	81B Dk. Colonial Brown	801
©	51C Gold Brown	436
⊙	143 Lt. Cardinal	815
∇	90A Bright Gold	783
⊞	5A Chartreuse	704
⊠	37 Dk. Lavender	554
Ⓤ	267 Lt. Salmon	754
3	231 Goldenrod	742
Ⓛ	75A Tropic Orange	920
■	36 Royal Purple	550
Ⓢ	109 Dk. Willow Green	367
☐	Fabric as is	

Backstitch Color Key

81B Dk. Colonial Brown		801
51C Gold Brown		436
143 Lt. Cardinal		815

Purchase 3 skeins each of 62 Russet, 51C Gold Brown, 120 Crimson, and DMC 642. Purchase 2 skeins each of 81B Dk. Colonial Brown and 75A Tropic Orange. Buy 1 skein of each remaining color.

To find the starting point of the first cross-stitch: Measure across 3 1/2" from top left corner; measure downwards 3 1/8" from top left corner. Mark the point where these two measurements intersect. Start embroidering the first row on the mushroom in upper left corner that is a combination of gold brown, purple, beige, and chartreuse.

Areas of special concern: Change the names, births, marriages, deaths, and signature lines. For signature line, see alphabet no. 2. Use alphabet no. 6 for other letters. For numerals, see numerals no 1. There are 106 spaces in width to work with under the names heading. There are 45 spaces in width

to work with under the births, marriages, and deaths headings. And there are 256 spaces in width to work with on the signature line (line extends from start of names to end of deaths column—that leaves a minimum of at least 3 spaces on either side). "Family Register," "names," births," "marriages," and "deaths" headings stay as and where they are. The decorative hearts (and details on each side) in the marriage column, and the double curves in the death column are centered as they should be, if needed. Leave 1 space between each letter within a word, between each number within a date, between months and a period, and between days and a comma. Leave 5 spaces between each full word, between words and numbers, and between complete dates. Pretend periods and commas do not exist when figuring out spacing between months and days and between days and years. Under marriages heading, if person is not married, just use hearts without details on each side. Names, births, marriages, and deaths are aligned at the same distance from the left margin. Center the signature line.

Note: Under the names heading, there are spaces for twelve family members. My column includes (from top to bottom) my name, my husband's name, names of my mother and father, names of my maternal grandparents, names of my paternal grandparents, names of my maternal great-grandparents, and names of my paternal great-grandparents.

Area of backstitch (indicated by bold lines on charted graph): *81B Dk. Colonial Brown*—veins on biggest yellow leaf and on chartreuse leaf. *51C Gold Brown*—vein on smallest yellow leaf. *143 Lt. Cardinal*—line on underside of one mushroom.

Margin to be added when mounting: Add 7/8" borders on all four sides of the embroidery.

Illus. 37. Charted graph for "Family Register."

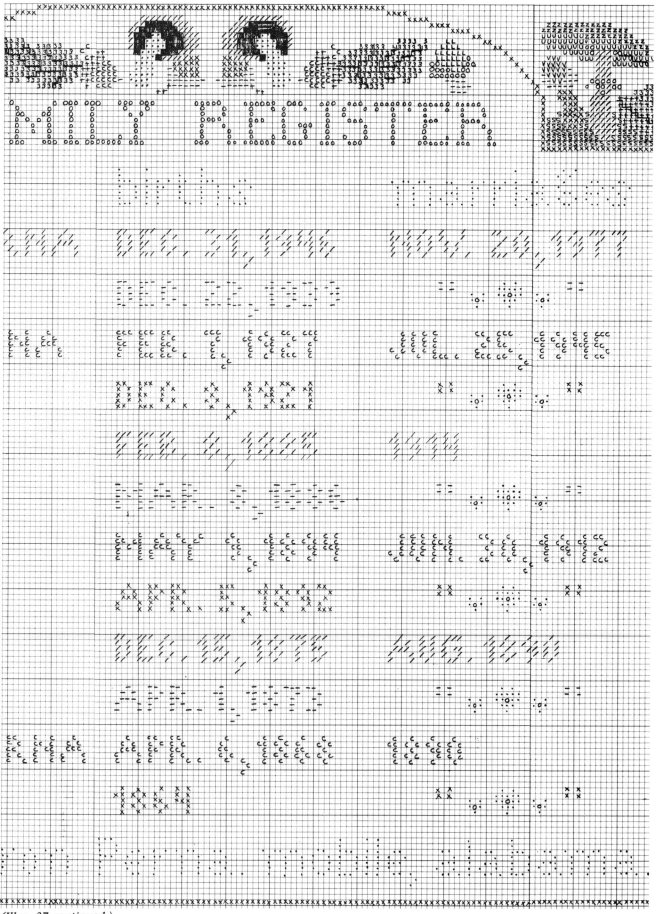

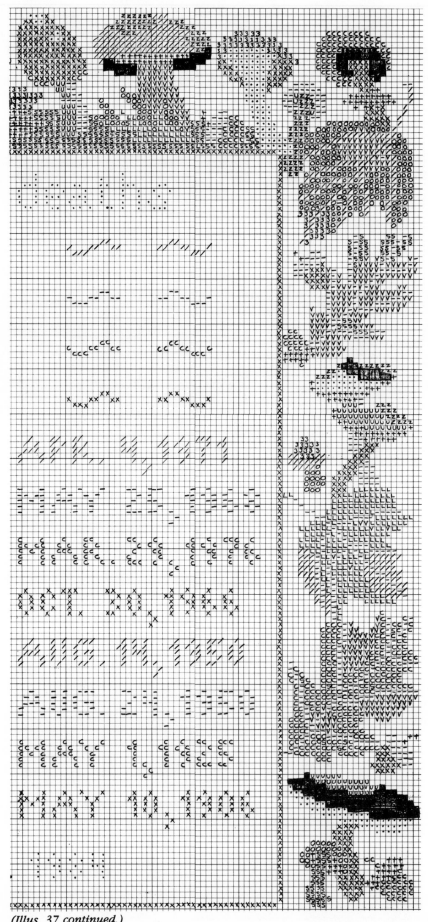

(Illus. 37 continued.)

Alphabet Samplers

Town

(Color page E)

Degree of work: easy
Fabric: ivory aida (11 count)
Cut size of fabric needed: 20" wide x 16"
Finished size: approximately 16" x 12"

Cross-Stitch Color Key

Symbol	J. & P. Coats six-strand floss	or DMC six-strand floss
⊠	81B Dk. Colonial Brown	801
⊡	216 Avocado	469
⧄	143 Lt. Cardinal	815
◆	90A Bright Gold	783
▣	1 White	Snow-White
3	Use DMC 642	642
L	75A Tropic Orange	920
△	51C Gold Brown	436
☐	Fabric as is	

Illus. 38.

Purchase 2 skeins of 81B Dk. Colonial Brown. Buy 1 skein of each remaining color.

To find the starting point of the first cross-stitch: Measure across 3 3/4" from top left corner; measure downwards 3" from top left corner. Mark the point where these two measurements intersect. Start embroidering the small avocado colored leaf in top left corner.

Margin to be added when mounting: Add 1 1/2" borders on all four sides of the embroidery.

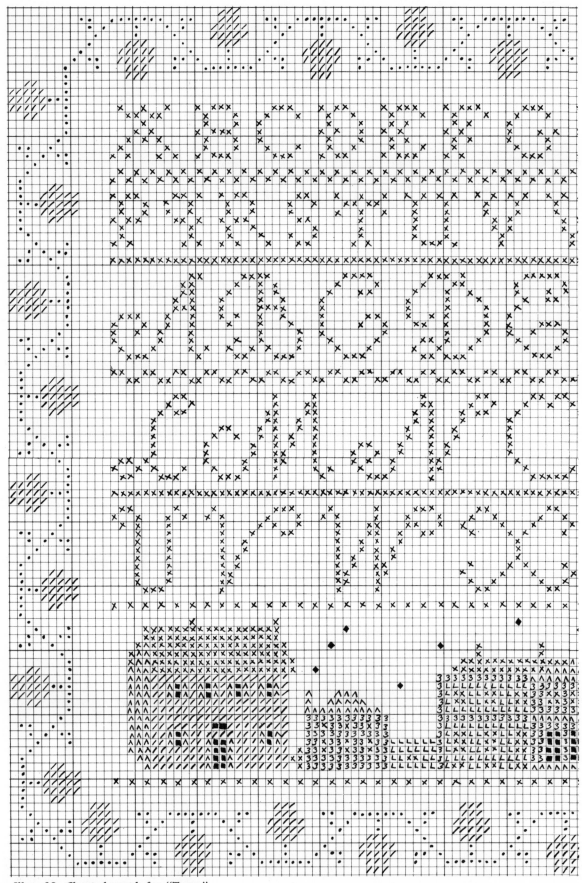

Illus. 39. Charted graph for "Town."

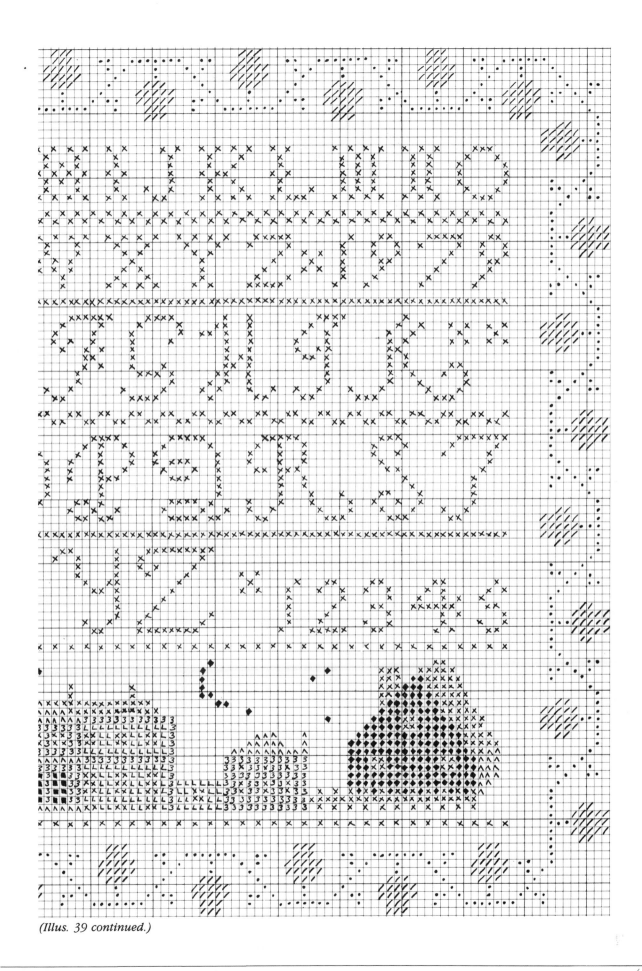

(Illus. 39 continued.)

Chipmunk among the Vegetables

(Color page F)

Degree of work: moderate
Fabric: white aida (11 count)
Cut size of fabric needed: 17 1/2" wide x 20"
Finished size: approximately 12 3/4" x 15 1/2"

Illus. 40.

Cross-Stitch Color Key

Symbol	J. & P. Coats six-strand floss	or DMC six-strand floss
L	140 Signal Red	321
·	5A Chartreuse	704
C	143 Lt. Cardinal	815
e	90A Bright Gold	783
N	36 Royal Purple	550
■	100 Fast Red	816
U	38B Tangerine	947
E	81 Dk. Brown	434
⊠	28 Myrtle	700
S	99 Grass Green	703
◆	62 Russet	435
◢	81B Dk. Colonial Brown	801
O	26 Nile Green	966
▯	12 Black	310
◮	213 Beige	644
♥	1 White	Snow-White
M	32 Purple	552
◿	37 Dk. Lavender	554
3	38 Dk. Orange	741
Q	216 Avocado	469
◰	75A Tropic Orange	920
T	9 Yellow	745
☐	Fabric as is	

Purchase 3 skeins of 28 Myrtle and 2 skeins of 5A Chartreuse. Buy 1 skein of each remaining color.

To find the starting point of the first cross-stitch: Measure across 3" from top left corner; measure downwards 3" from top left corner. Mark the point where these two measurements intersect. Start embroidering the first lavender stitch in top row.

Margin to be added when mounting: Add 1" borders on all four sides of the embroidery.

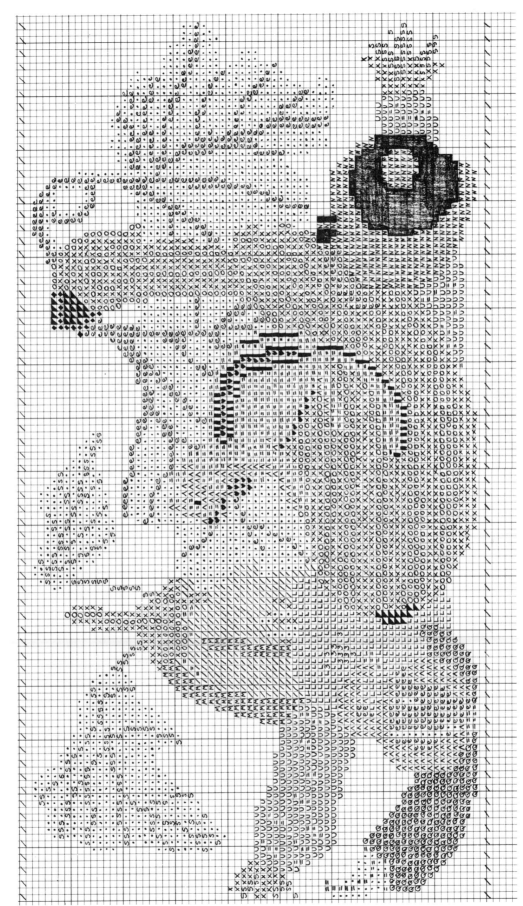

Illus. 41. Charted graph for "Chipmunk among the Vegetables."

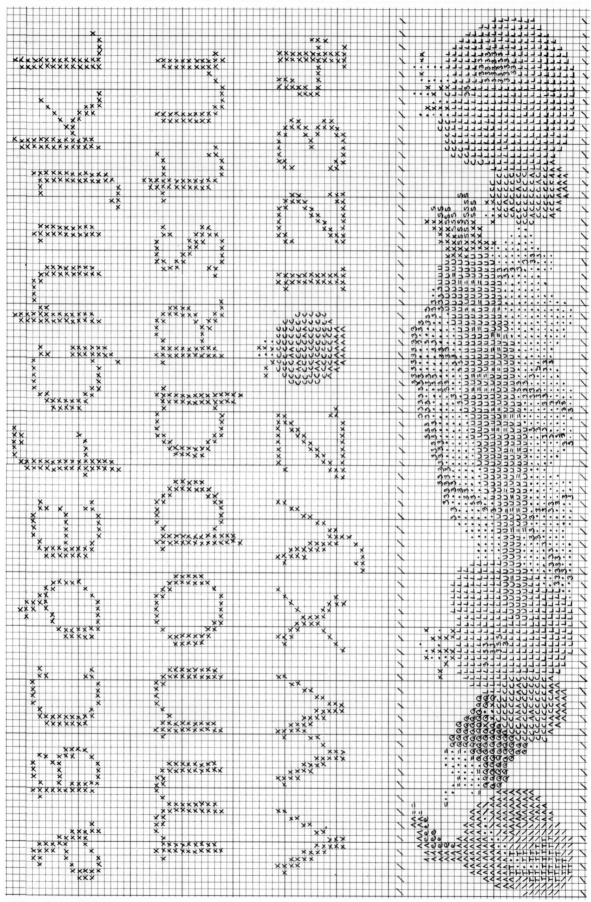

(Illus. 41 continued.)

Watermelons

Illus. 42.

Degree of work: challenging
Fabric: white aida (11 count)
Cut size of fabric needed: 24" wide x 22"
Finished size: approximately 18 3/8" x 17 1/8"

Cross-Stitch Color Key

Symbol	J. & P. Coats six-strand floss	or DMC six-strand floss
☒	48A Dk. Hunter's Green	701
⧄	122 Watermelon	961
U	12 Black	310
■	1 White	Snow-White
3	100 Fast Red	816
▲	51C Gold Brown	436
=	28 Myrtle	700
O	26 Nile Green	966
☐	Fabric as is	

Backstitch Color Key

⊞	12 Black	310

Purchase 5 skeins of 48A Dk. Hunter's Green, 4 skeins of 26 Nile Green, 3 skeins each of 12 Black and 122 Watermelon, and 2 skeins of 28 Myrtle. Buy 1 skein of each remaining color.

To find the starting point of the first cross-stitch: Measure across 3 3/8" from top left corner; measure downwards 3" from top left corner. Mark the point where these two measurements intersect. Start embroidering the first black diamond in top row.

Areas of special concern: Watch the outer watermelon border. There are 2 spaces between the watermelon repeats on the top and bottom. There is 1 space between the watermelon repeats on the sides.

Area of backstitch (indicated by bold lines on charted graph): *12 Black*—all vines and watermelon pits on outside border.

Margin to be added when mounting: Add 3/4" borders on all four sides of the embroidery.

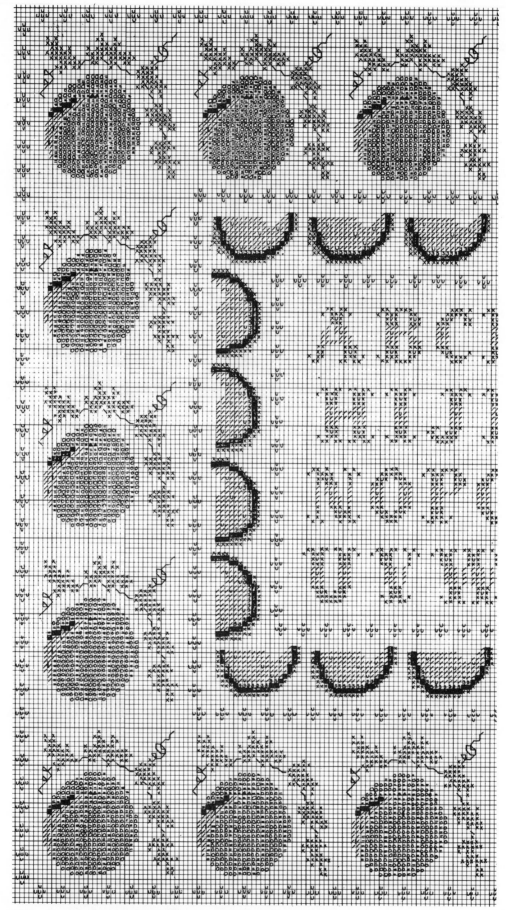

Illus. 43. Charted graph for "Watermelons."

(Illus. 43 continued.)

Flower Basket

Degree of work: challenging
Fabric: ivory aida (11 count)
Cut size of fabric needed: 21 1/2'' wide x 24 1/2''
Finished size: approximately 16 3/4'' x 20''

Cross-Stitch Color Key

Symbol	J. & P. Coats six-strand floss	or DMC six-strand floss
⊠	245 Atlantic Blue	799
⧄	120 Crimson	351
L	261 Wild Honey	436
c	81 Dk. Brown	434
e	61 Ecru	822
◆	90A Bright Gold	783
V	81B Dk. Colonial Brown	801
•	Use DMC 642	642
O	5A Chartreuse	704
▢	75A Tropic Orange	920
S	1 White	Snow-White
■	223 Sun Gold	743
U	109 Dk. Willow Green	367
⧄	69 Lt. Steel Blue	809
⊟	124 Indian Pink	353
3	143 Lt. Cardinal	815
⧅	28 Myrtle	700
T	36 Royal Purple	550
M	54 Violet	553
▢	Fabric as is	

Backstitch Color Key

⊞	109 Dk. Willow Green	367
	28 Myrtle	700
	143 Lt. Cardinal	815
	120 Crimson	351
	81B Dk. Colonial Brown	801
	36 Royal Purple	550

Purchase 4 skeins of 245 Atlantic Blue and 2 skeins each of 261 Wild Honey, 81B Dk. Colonial Brown, 5A Chartreuse, and 109 Dk. Willow Green. Buy 1 skein of each remaining color.

Illus. 44.

To find the starting point of the first cross-stitch: Measure across 3'' from top left corner; measure downwards 3'' from top left corner. Mark the point where these two measurements intersect. Start embroidering the first row on small leaf (dark willow green) in upper left corner.

Area of backstitch (indicated by bold lines on charted graph): *109 Dk. Willow Green*—bud and leaf stems on morning glory border; bud and leaf stems on left blue morning glory in the basket. *28 Myrtle*—two feathery leaves and stem on left side of basket. *143 Lt. Cardinal*—lines acting as petal separations within crimson flower. *120 Crimson*—line acting as petal separation within Indian pink flower. *81B Dk. Colonial Brown*—Short lines on basket rim. *36 Royal Purple*—veins on both pansies.

Margin to be added when mounting: Add 3/4'' borders on all four sides of the embroidery.

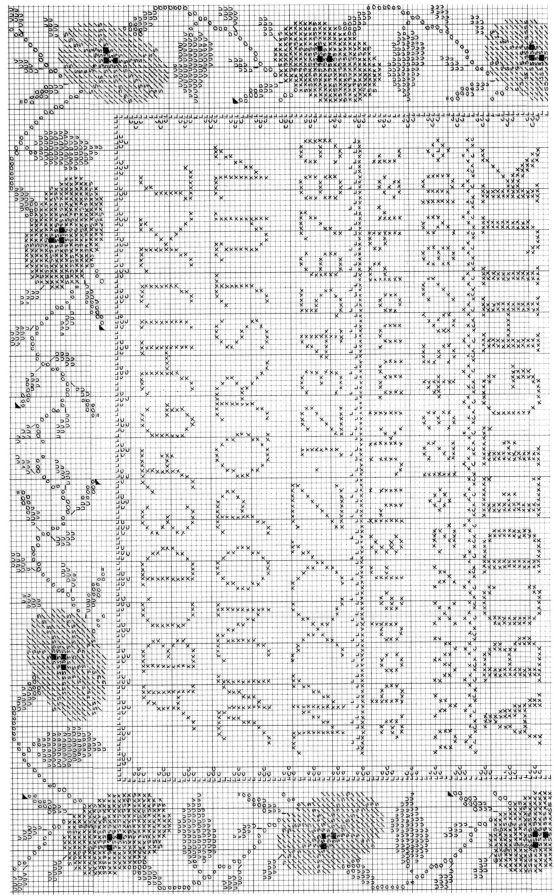

Illus. 45. Charted graph for "Flower Basket."

(Illus. 45 continued.)

Swans

Degree of work: challenging
Fabric: white aida (11 count)
Cut size of fabric needed: 21" wide x 20 1/2"
Finished size: approximately 16 5/8" x 16"

Cross-Stitch Color Key

Symbol	J. & P. Coats six-strand floss	or DMC six-strand floss
☒	12 Black	310
U	1 White	Snow-White
S	140 Signal Red	321
3	Use DMC 414	414
·	245 Atlantic Blue	799
O	71 Pewter Grey	415
T	81 Dk. Brown	434
■	26 Nile Green	966
◆	235 Mint Gold	782
M	216 Avocado	469
L	76 China Blue	825
–	24A Oriental Blue	518
☐	Fabric as is	

Backstitch Color Key

▦	12 Black	310

Purchase 6 skeins of 12 Black and 2 skeins each of 245 Atlantic Blue, 71 Pewter Grey, 76 China Blue, and 24A Oriental Blue. Buy 1 skein of each remaining color.

To find the starting point of the first cross-stitch: Measure across 3" from top left corner; measure downwards 3" from top left corner. Mark

Illus. 46.

the point where these two measurements intersect. Start embroidering the first blue stitch on the border corner.

Areas of special concern: On second and third horizontal bands of different swan designs, each central swan has one more stitch (in middle of back) than the swans on either side.

Area of backstitch (indicated by bold lines on charted graph): *12 Black*—all cattail stems.

Margin to be added when mounting: Add 1" borders on all four sides of the embroidery.

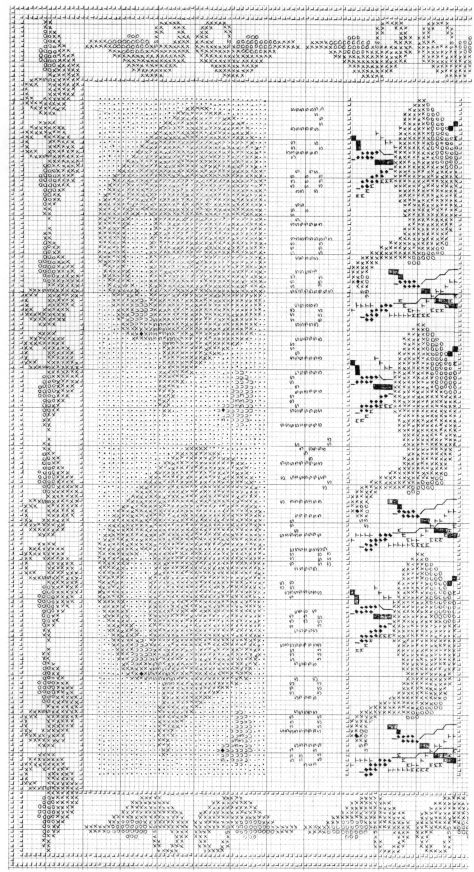

*Illus. 47. Charted graph
for "Swans."*

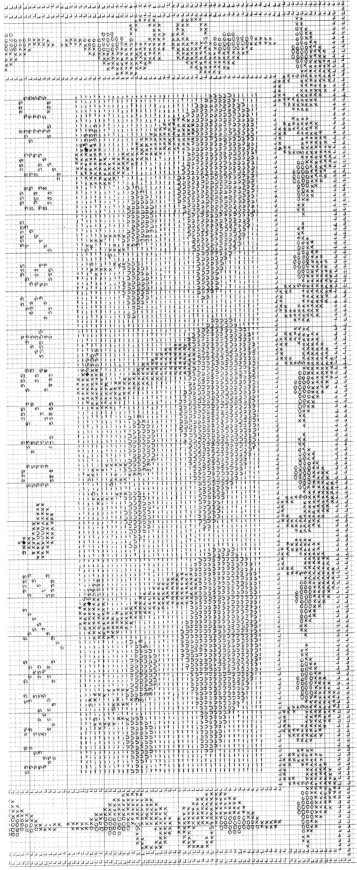

(Illus. 47 continued.)

Verse Samplers

The Early Bird Catches the Worm

(Color page H)

Degree of work: easy
Fabric: ivory aida (11 count)
Cut size of fabric needed: 20" wide x 18"
Finished size: approximately 15" x 13 1/4"

Cross-Stitch Color Key

Symbol	J. & P. Coats six-strand floss	or DMC six-strand floss
S	141 Devil Red	666
3	61 Ecru	822
+	62 Russet	435
■	12 Black	310
O	143 Lt. Cardinal	815
•	267 Lt. Salmon	754
=	Use DMC 642	642
Z	81B Dk. Colonial Brown	801
/	109 Dk. Willow Green	367
△	5A Chartreuse	704
X	90A Bright Gold	783
□	Fabric as is	

Backstitch Color Key

⊞	12 Black	310
	143 Lt. Cardinal	815

Purchase 2 skeins each of 62 Russet, 81B Dk. Colonial Brown, and 109 Dk. Willow Green. Buy 1 skein of each remaining color.

Illus. 48.

To find the starting point of the first cross-stitch: Measure across 3 1/4" from top left corner; measure downwards 3 1/8" from top left corner. Mark the point where these two measurements intersect. Start embroidering the light salmon flower in the top left corner.

Area of backstitch (indicated by bold lines on charted graph): *12 Black*—line within all dark red berries; and numbers on clock. *143 Lt. Cardinal*—the ends on both clock hands.

Margin to be added when mounting: Add 1" borders on all four sides of the embroidery.

Illus. 49. (Opposite) Charted graph for "The Early Bird Catches the Worm."

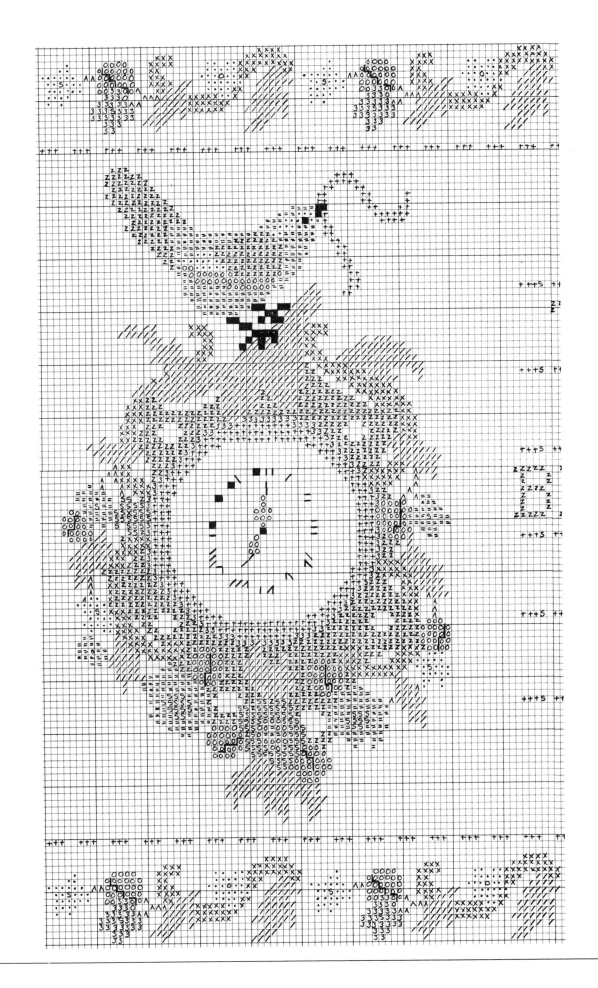

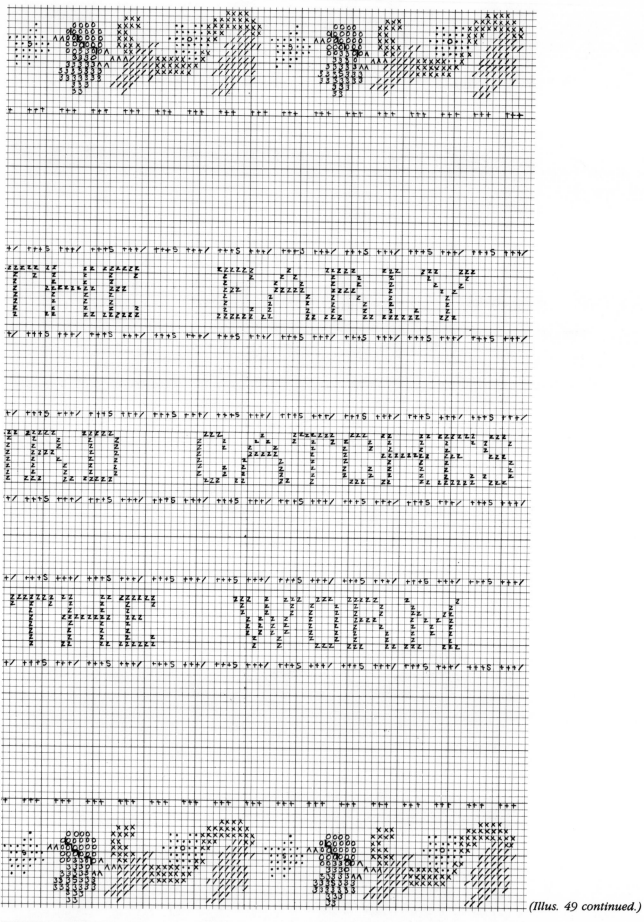

(Illus. 49 continued.)

Don't Count Your Chickens

(Color page I)

Degree of work: easy
Fabric: ivory aida (11 count)
Cut size of fabric needed: 18" wide x 24"
Finished size: approximately 14 1/4" x 19 1/2"

Illus. 50.

Cross-Stitch Color Key

Symbol	J. & P. Coats six-strand floss	or DMC six-strand floss
S	222 Dk. Aquatone	597
O	38 Dk. Orange	741
X	140 Signal Red	321
▲	38B Tangerine	947
—	81B Dk. Colonial Brown	801
•	253 Daffodil	444
■	143 Lt. Cardinal	815
Z	51C Gold Brown	436
/	267 Lt. Salmon	754
3	61 Ecru	822
U	266 Fleshtone	951
∧	24B Dk. Oriental Blue	806
e	75A Tropic Orange	920
☐	Fabric as is	

Purchase 2 skeins of 140 Signal Red. Buy 1 skein of each remaining color.

To find the starting point of the first cross-stitch: Measure across 3 1/2" from top left corner; measure downwards 3" from top left corner. Mark the point where these two measurements intersect. Start embroidering the first red cross-stitch in top left corner of design.

Margin to be added when mounting: Add 1" borders on all four sides of the embroidery.

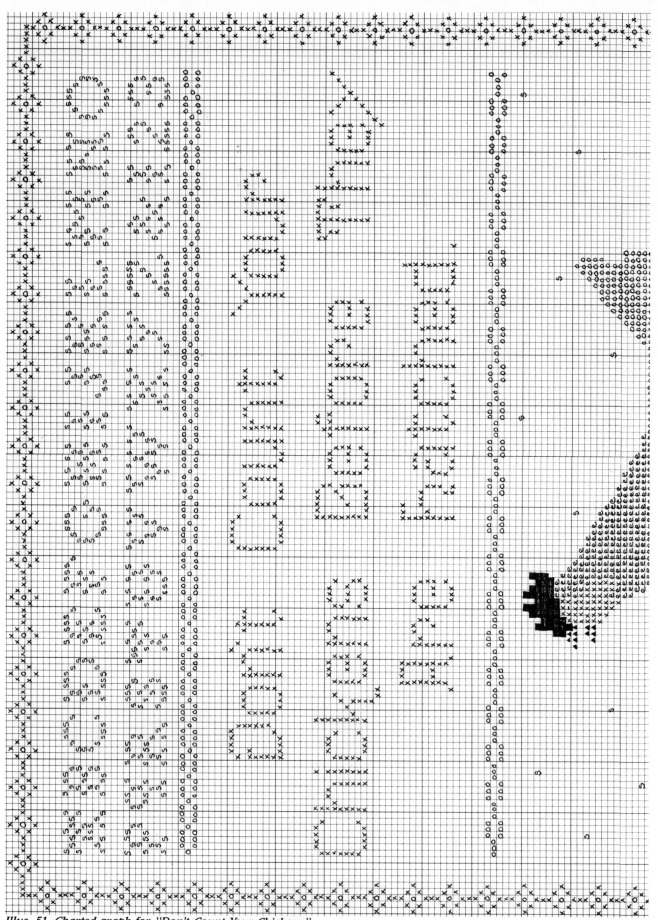

Illus. 51. Charted graph for "Don't Count Your Chickens."

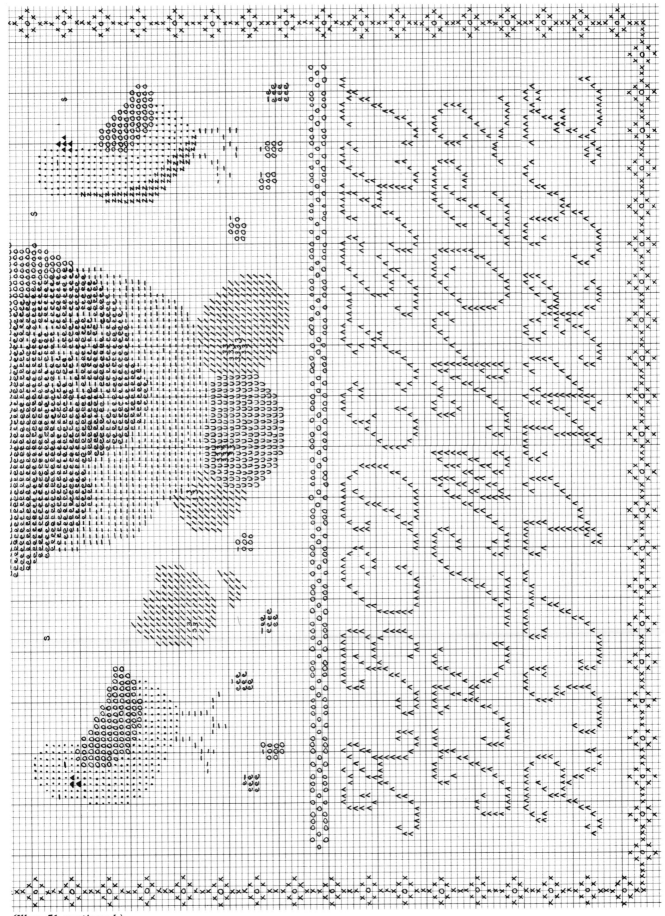

(Illus. 51 continued.)

Home Sweet Home

Illus. 52.

Degree of work: easy
Fabric: ivory aida (11 count)
Cut size of fabric needed: 27" wide x 14"
Finished size: approximately 22 3/8" x 9 5/8"

Cross-Stitch Color Key

Symbol	J. & P. Coats six-strand floss	or DMC six-strand floss
⊠	28 Myrtle	700
•	26 Nile Green	966
3	5A Chartreuse	704
=	223 Sun Gold	743
■	75A Tropic Orange	920
∕	62 Russet	435
5	81B Dk. Colonial Brown	801
O	38 Dk. Orange	741
☐	Fabric as is	

Backstitch Color Key

⊞	81B Dk. Colonial Brown	801

Purchase 2 skeins each of 28 Myrtle and 26 Nile Green.
Buy 1 skein of each remaining color.

To find the starting point of the first cross-stitch: Measure across 3" from top left corner; measure downwards 3" from top left corner. Mark the point where these two measurements intersect. Start embroidering the first chartreuse stitch at top of decorative curve in upper left corner

Area of backstitch (indicated by bold lines on charted graph): *81B Dk. Colonial Brown*—middle of each daisy.

Margin to be added when mounting: Add 1" borders on all four sides of the embroidery. In this instance, measure from outside of the light green rectangle; ignore the decorative curves on the corners.

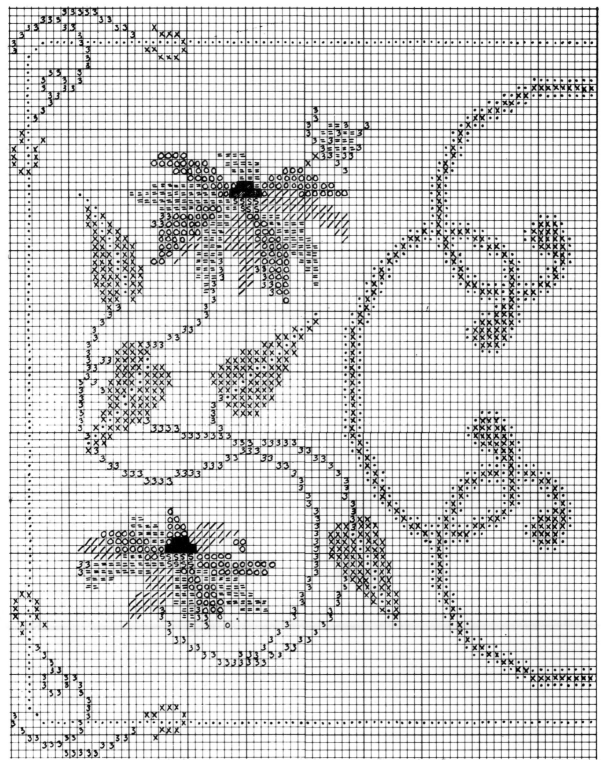

Illus. 53. Charted graph for "Home Sweet Home."

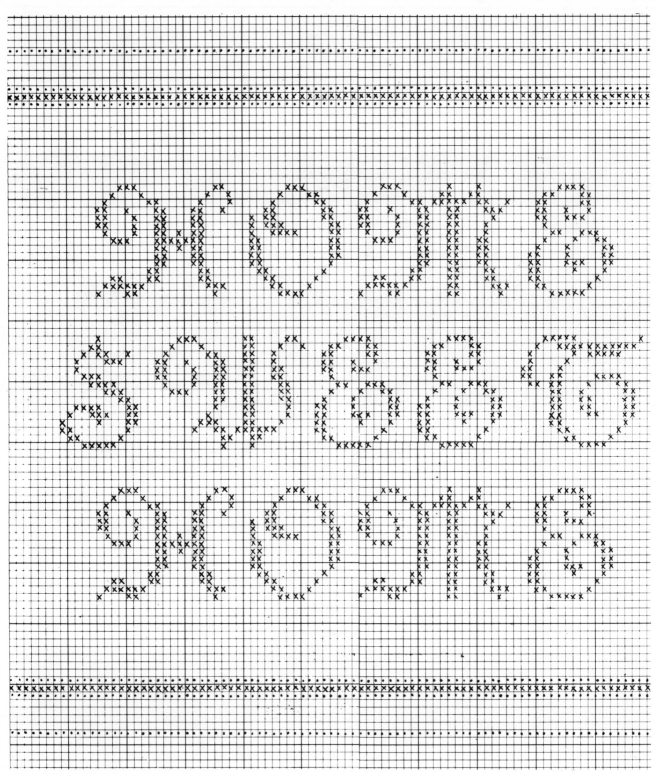

(Illus. 53 continued.)

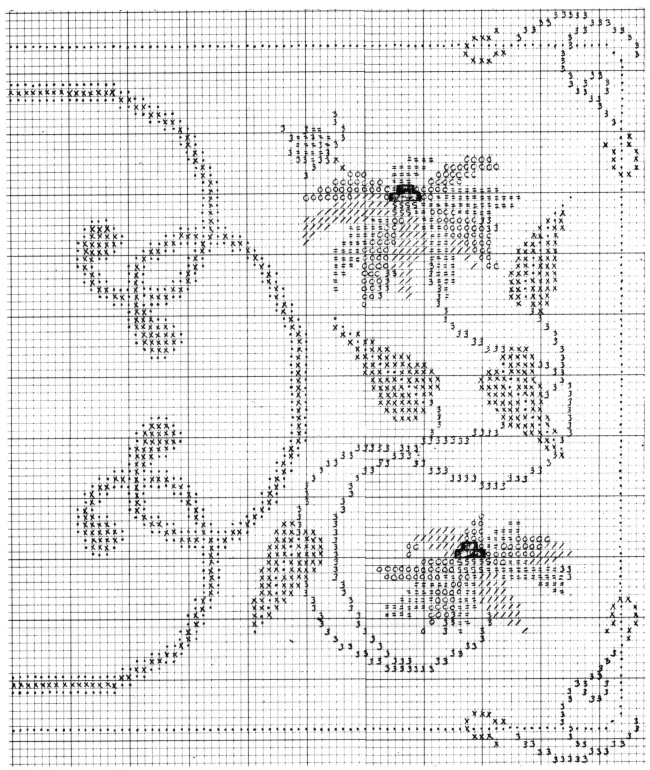

(Illus. 53 continued.)

Bless Our House

Degree of work: easy
Fabric: white aida (11 count)
Cut size of fabric needed: 17" wide x 15"
Finished size: approximately 12 1/8" x 10 1/2"

Cross-Stitch Color Key

Symbol	J. & P. Coats six-strand floss	or DMC six-strand floss
☒	28 Myrtle	700
⊡	5A Chartreuse	704
⊙	1 White	Snow-White
☑	223 Sun Gold	743
■	12 Black	310
◪	Use DMC 414	414
⑨	81 Dk. Brown	434
◺	75A Tropic Orange	920
≡	90A Bright Gold	783
◆	70 Silver Grey	762
⊞	99 Grass Green	703
Q	Use DMC 642	642
◩	8 Blue	800
▲	69 Lt. Steel Blue	809
③	9 Yellow	745
M	210 Leaf Green	368
♥	26 Nile Green	966
C	226 Pearl Pink	963
L	124 Indian Pink	353
⑨	62 Russet	435
☐	Fabric as is	

Backstitch Color Key

⊞	12 Black	310
	1 White	Snow-White
	81 Dk. Brown	434
	90A Bright Gold	783
	223 Sun Gold	743
	Use DMC 414	414
	210 Leaf Green	368
	124 Indian Pink	353
	226 Pearl Pink	963

Purchase 2 skeins of 28 Myrtle. Buy 1 skein of each remaining color.

Illus. 54.

To find the starting point of the first cross-stitch: Measure across 6 1/2" from top left corner; measure downwards 3 1/4" from top left corner. Mark the point where these two measurements intersect. Start embroidering the single white cross-stitch at the top of roof on the yellow house.

Area of backstitch (indicated by bold lines on charted graph): *12 Black*—outline on all steps; all doorknobs; lines within all windows; top of chimney on yellow house; all decorative ironwork on blue house; roof on left side of pink house; and lamppost. *1 White*—decorative vertical lines near roof on yellow house. *81 Dk. Brown*—lines within sidewalk; roof and roof edges on yellow house; lines within dark green tree; and edges of dormer and roof on pink house. *90A Bright Gold*—Left edge of yellow house. *223 Sun Gold*—right edge of yellow house; and light in lamppost. *DMC 414*—roof and roof edges on blue house; vertical line between light and dark portions of blue house; roof edges on green house; and outline around bay windows on pink house; and vertical line on white trim in pink house. *210 Leaf Green*—right and left edges of green house. *124 Indian Pink*—right edge of pink house. *226 Pearl Pink*—lines between two windows on pink dormer.

Margin to be added at mounting: Add 1" borders on all four sides of the embroidery.

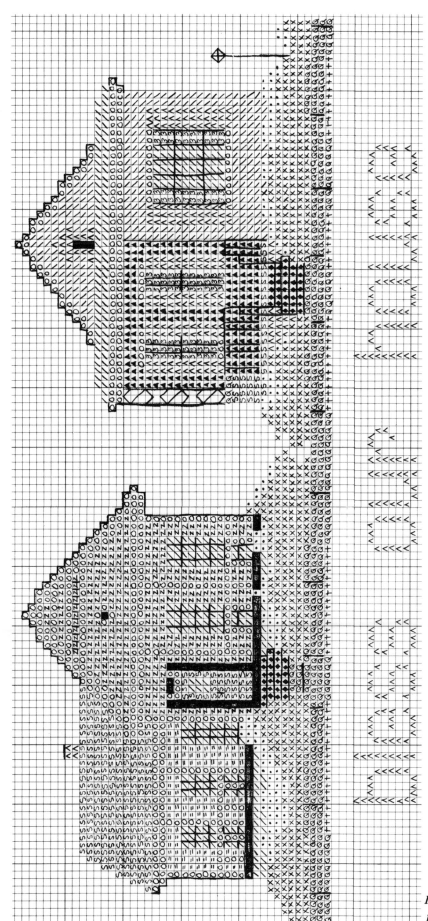

Illus. 55. Charted graph for "Bless Our House."

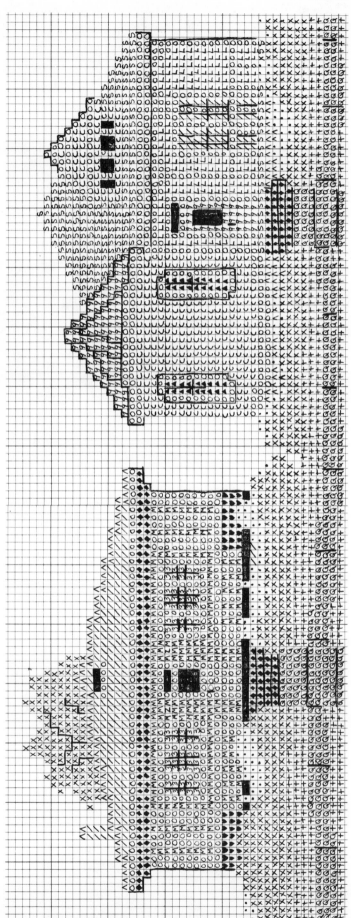

(Illus. 55 continued.)

Degree of work: moderate
Fabric: white aida (11 count)
Cut size of fabric needed: 17" wide x 21"
Finished size: approximately 12 7/8" x 16 1/8"

Cross-Stitch Color Key

Symbol	J. & P. Coats six-strand floss	or DMC six-strand floss
☒	81 Dk. Brown	434
⊟	51C Gold Brown	436
⊡	81B Dk. Colonial Brown	801
Ⓛ	28 Myrtle	700
③	48A Dk. Hunter's Green	701
ⓞ	5A Chartreuse	704
ⓢ	26 Nile Green	966
■	Use DMC 642	642
ⓒ	10A Canary Yellow	445
ⓩ	143 Lt. Cardinal	815
ⓔ	120 Crimson	351
Ⓤ	216 Avocado	469
⊞	43 Dk. Yellow	744
Ⓜ	90A Bright Gold	783
⧄	109 Dk. Willow Green	367
Ⓠ	223 Sun Gold	743
▲	61 Ecru	822
◨	141 Devil Red	666
◆	54 Violet	553
◺	36 Royal Purple	550
☐	Fabric as is	

Backstitch Color Key

⊞	81B Dk. Colonial Brown	801
	81 Dk. Brown	434
	5A Chartreuse	704
	143 Lt. Cardinal	815

Purchase 2 skeins of 81 Dk. Brown. Buy 1 skein of each remaining color.

Illus. 56.

To find the starting point of the first cross-stitch: Measure across 3 3/4" from top left corner; measure downwards 3 3/4" from top left corner. Mark the point where these two measurements intersect. Start embroidering the brown decorative flourish on the left; then continue with the "w."

Area of backstitch (indicated by bold lines on charted graph): *81B Dk. Colonial Brown*—on flourishes surrounding welcome and on stems for pear, peach, cherries, and grape leaves. *81 Dk. Brown*—on apple and plum stems. *5A Chartreuse*—on cherry stems that hang on vase. *143 Lt. Cardinal*—to outline pineapple sections.

Margin to be added when mounting: Add 7/8" borders on all four sides of the embroidery.

Illus. 57. Charted graph for "Welcome."

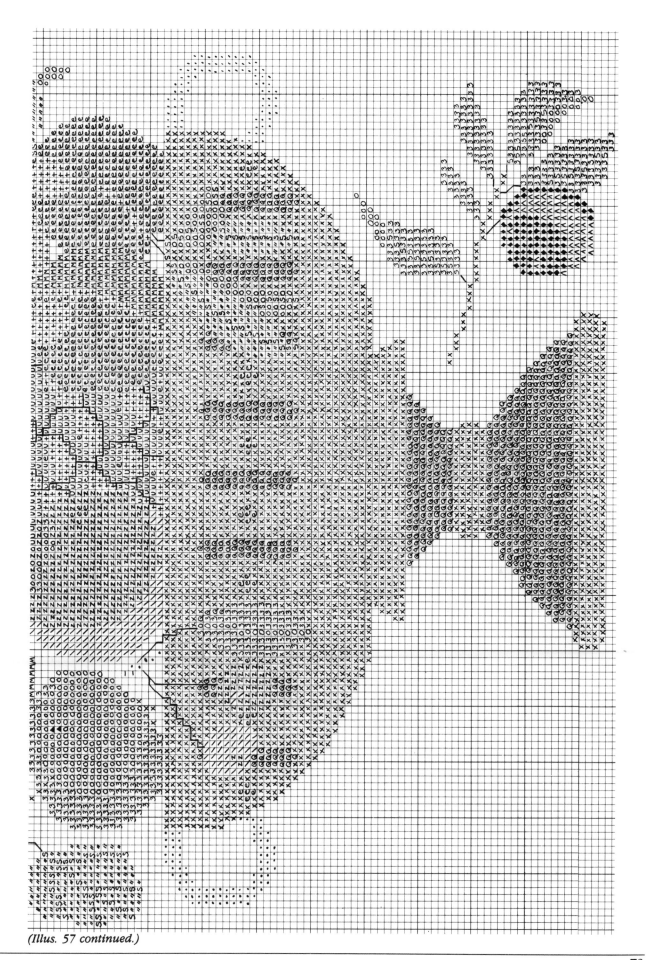

(Illus. 57 continued.)

Hurray for the Red, White, and Blue

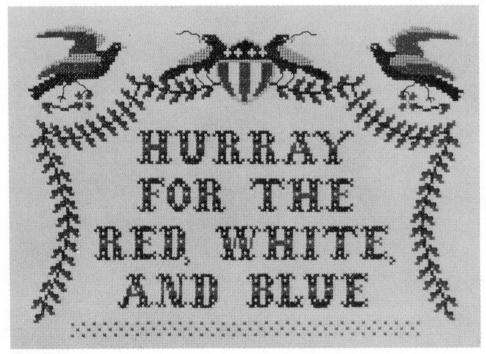

Illus. 58.

Degree of work: easy
Fabric: white aida (11 count)
Cut size of fabric needed: 20" wide x 16"
Finished size: approximately 15 1/4" x 11 3/8"

Cross-Stitch Color Key

Symbol	J. & P. Coats six-strand floss	or DMC six-strand floss
O	44 Royal Blue	796
X	140 Signal Red	321
S	1 White	Snow-White
U	69 Lt. Steel Blue	809
■	231 Goldenrod	742
=	55 Navy	823
☐	Fabric as is	

Backstitch Color Key

⊞	44 Royal Blue	796

Purchase 2 skeins each of 44 Royal Blue and 140 Signal Red. Buy 1 skein of each remaining color.

To find the starting point of the first cross-stitch: Measure across 4" from top left corner; measure downwards 3" from top left corner. Mark the point where these two measurements intersect. Start embroidering the first light blue cross-stitch at very top of the bird's wing (red and blue bird on the left side).

Area of backstitch (indicated by bold lines on charted graph): *44 Royal Blue*—all areas.

Margin to be added when mounting: Add 1" borders on all four sides of the embroidery.

Illus. 59. (Opposite) Charted graph for "Hurray for the Red, White, and Blue."

(Illus. 59 continued.)

Merry Christmas

Degree of work: moderate
Fabric: white aida (11 count)
Cut size of fabric needed: 17" wide x 19 1/2"
Finished size: approximately 12 5/8" x 14 3/4"

Cross-Stitch Color Key

Symbol	J. & P. Coats six-strand floss	or DMC six-strand floss
•	245 Atlantic Blue	798
S	1 White	Snow-White
⊠	28 Myrtle	700
■	98 Fern Green	989
O	140 Signal Red	321
▲	143 Lt. Cardinal	815
3	71 Pewter Grey	762
♥	59B Dk. Pink	899
T	4A Mid Rose	818
K	266 Fleshtone	951
=	261 Wild Honey	436
U	81A Colonial Brown	433
A	12 Black	310
◨	Use DMC 775	775
◢	46A Mid Rose	3326
Z	11 Orange	972
☐	Fabric as is	

Backstitch Color Key

🔳	12 Black	310

Purchase 2 skeins each of 245 Atlantic Blue, 28 Myrtle, and 140 Signal Red. Buy 1 skein of each remaining color.

To find the starting point of the first cross-stitch: Measure across 3" from top left corner; measure downwards 3" from top left corner. Mark the point where these two measurements intersect. Start embroidering the first bright red berry in the top left corner.

Illus. 60.

Areas of special concern: Change the date and initials. See alphabet no. 14 and numerals no. 11. There are 47 spaces in width to work with (that leaves a minimum of 2 spaces at the beginning of the date and a minimum of 2 spaces at the end of the punctuation). Leave 2 spaces between each numeral within a date, between date and decorative square, between decorative square and first initial, and between period and second initial. After each initial, leave 1 space; then make a period. Center the line.

Area of backstitch (indicated by bold lines on charted graph): *12 Black*—all areas.

Margin to be added when mounting: Add 1" borders on all four sides of the embroidery.

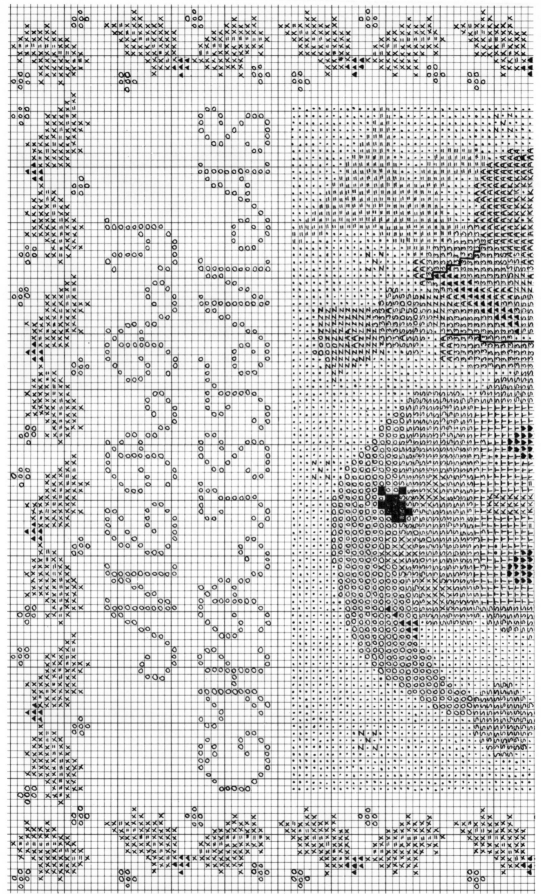

Illus. 61. Charted graph for "Merry Christmas."

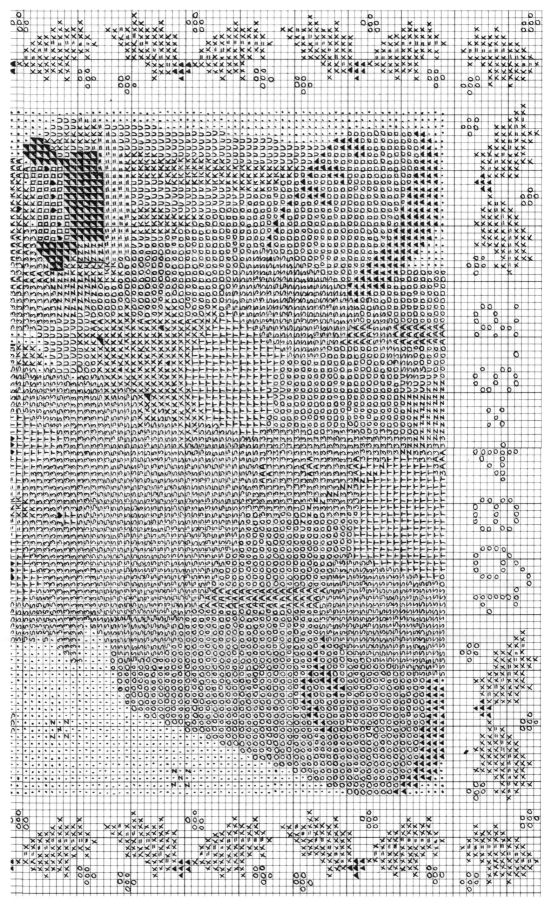

(Illus. 61 continued.)

Love One Another

Illus. 62.

Degree of work: easy
Fabric: white aida (11 count)
Cut size of fabric needed: 25" wide x 17"
Finished size: approximately 19" x 10 3/4"

Cross-Stitch Color Key

Symbol	J. & P. Coats six-strand floss	or DMC six-strand floss
⊠	140 Signal Red	321
·	218 Coral Glow	893
L	216 Avocado	469
◪	26 Nile Green	966
e	143 Lt. Cardinal	815
▲	46A Mid Rose	3326
3	28B Treeleaf Green	991
■	4A Mid Pink	818
O	122 Watermelon	961
☐	Fabric as is	

Buy 1 skein of each color.

To find the starting point of the first cross-stitch: Measure across 4 1/2" from top left corner; measure downwards 4 1/4" from top left corner. Mark the point where two measurements intersect. Start embroidering the first row of the dark green leaf in top left corner.

Areas of special concern: Change the name and date. See alphabet no. 6 and numerals no. 1. There are 114 spaces in width to work with (exact length of heart repeat). "Love One," "Another," and the heart repeat stay as and where they are. Leave 1 space between each letter within a word and between each number within a date. Leave 5 spaces between each complete word and between word and date. Do not count the centered cross-stitch that separates the name and date. Center line.

Margin to be added when mounting: Add 1 1/8" borders on all four sides of the embroidery.

Illus. 63. Charted graph for "Love One Another."

(Illus. 63 continued.)

God Is Love

Illus. 64.

Degree of work: easy
Fabric: ivory aida (11 count)
Cut size of fabric needed: 20" wide x 17"
Finished size: approximately 15 3/8" x 11 3/4"

Cross-Stitch Color Key

Symbol	J. & P. Coats six-strand floss	or DMC six-strand floss
⊠	Use DMC 642	642
⦿	213 Beige	644
◺	69 Lt. Steel Blue	809
■	120 Crimson	351
Z	245 Atlantic Blue	798
♥	90A Bright Gold	783
3	32 Purple	552
•	124 Indian Pink	353
+	48A Dk. Hunter's Green	701
▲	28B Treeleaf Green	991
☐	Fabric as is	

Purchase 4 skeins of DMC 642 and 2 skeins of 213 Beige.
Buy 1 skein of each remaining color.

To find the starting point of the first cross-stitch: Measure across 3 1/2" from top left corner; measure downwards 3" from top left corner. Mark the point where these two measurements intersect. Start embroidering the four beige cross-stitches grouped in row one in the top left corner of the design.

Margin to be added when mounting: Add 13/16" borders on all four sides of the embroidery.

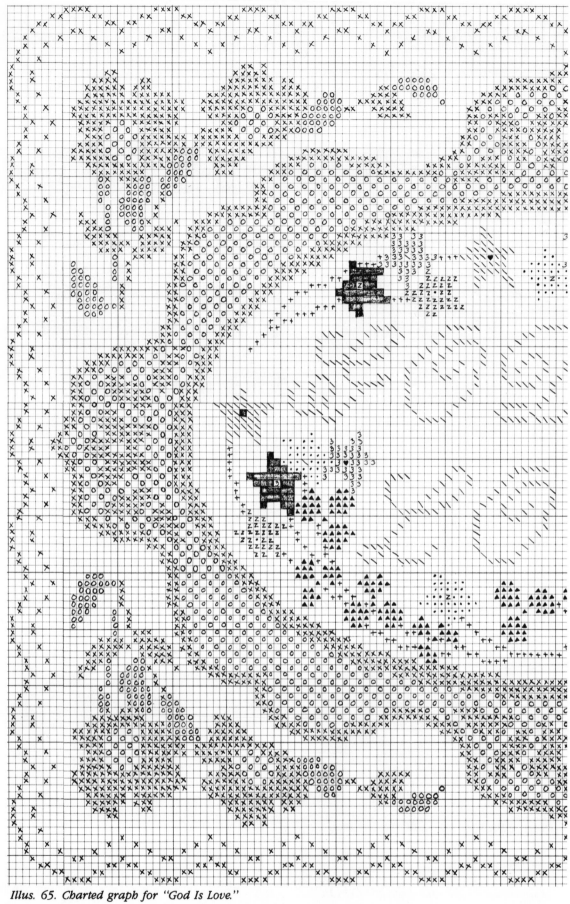

Illus. 65. Charted graph for "God Is Love."

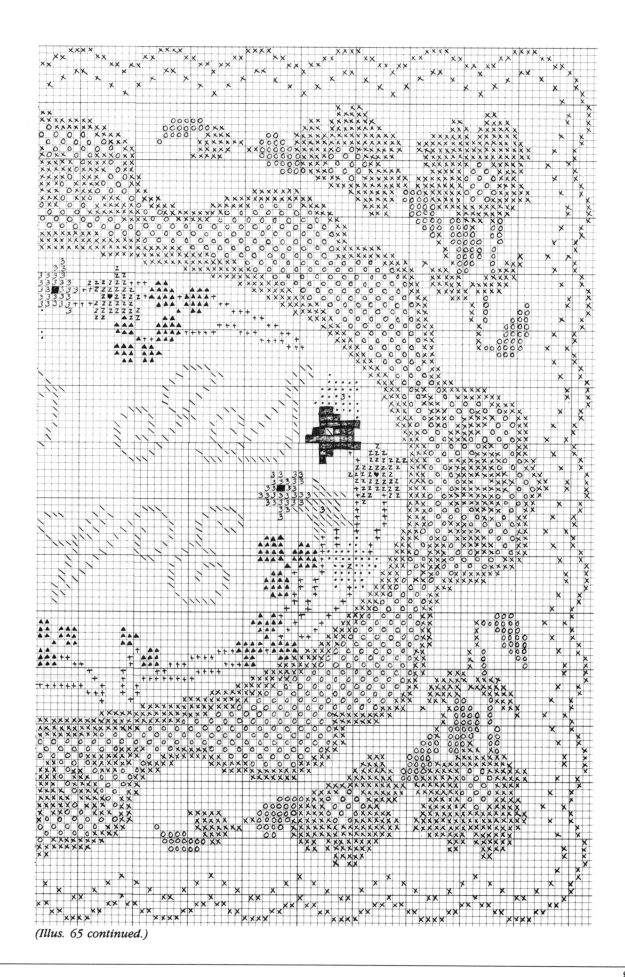

(Illus. 65 continued.)

Give Us Our Daily Bread

Degree of work: moderate
Fabric: ivory aida (11 count)
Cut size of fabric needed: 21" x 21"
Finished size: approximately 15 7/8" x 15 7/8"

Cross-Stitch Color Key

Symbol	J. & P. Coats six-strand floss	or DMC six-strand floss
△	81A Colonial Brown	433
⊠	28B Treeleaf Green	991
Ⓢ	26 Nile Green	966
ⓞ	124 Indian Pink	353
Ⓘ ⊟	75A Tropic Orange	920
ⓔ	Use DMC 642	642
▲	61 Ecru	822
■	36 Royal Purple	550
Ⓩ	81B Dk. Colonial Brown	801
③	90A Bright Gold	783
◪	1 White	Snow-White
Ⓤ	266 Fleshtone	951
◩	261 Wild Honey	436
Ⓣ	267 Lt. Salmon	754
Ⓛ	9 Yellow	745
☐	Fabric as is	

Backstitch Color Key

⊞	81A Colonial Brown	433
	Use DMC 642	642
	26 Nile Green	966
	81B Dk. Colonial Brown	801

Purchase 2 skeins each of 81A Colonial Brown, 28B Treeleaf Green, and 75A Tropic Orange. Buy 1 skein of each remaining color.

To find the starting point of the first cross-stitch: Measure across 3 1/2" from top left corner; measure downwards 3 3/4" from top left corner. Mark the point where these two measurements intersect. On the repeat border, start embroidering the

Illus. 66.

seven, dark green, horizontal cross-stitches grouped together in row eight of the top left corner.

Areas of special concern: Change the signature line. See alphabet no. 15 and numerals no. 7. There are 161 spaces in width to work with (exact length of cross-stitch lines above and below the name line). "Give Us Our" and "Daily Bread" stay as and where they they are. Leave 1 space between each letter within a word and between numbers within a date. Leave 5 spaces between complete words and numbers. Center the line.

Area of backstitch (indicated by bold lines on charted graph): *81A Colonial Brown*—wheat border and wheat in central design. *DMC 642*—bird's legs and outline around egg. *26 Nile Green*—leaves in bird's mouth. *81B Dk. Colonial Brown*—outline around loaf of bread.

Margin to be added when mounting: Add 3/4" borders on all four sides of the embroidery.

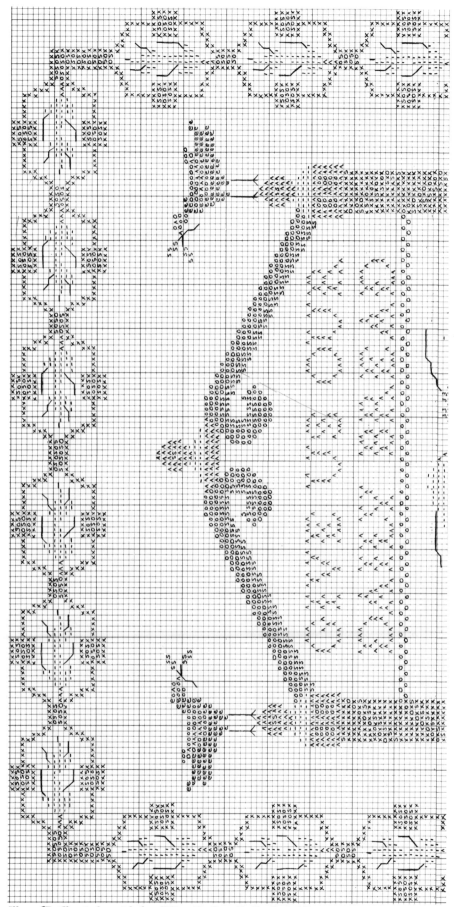

Illus. 67. Charted graph for "Give Us Our Daily Bread."

(Illus. 67 continued.)

Count Your Blessings

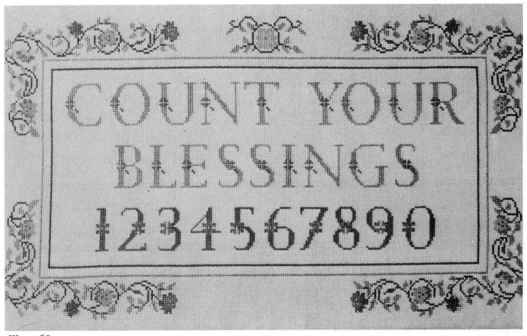

Illus. 68.

Degree of work: moderate
Fabric: white aida (11 count)
Cut size of fabric needed: 30" wide x 20"
Finished size: approximately 25" x 14 3/4"

Cross-Stitch Color Key

Symbol	J. & P. Coats six-strand floss	or DMC six-strand floss
·	215 Apple Green	471
T	75A Tropic Orange	920
O	253 Daffodil	444
=	32 Purple	552
X	28 Myrtle	700
S	81 Dk. Brown	434
◆	124 Indian Pink	353
☐	Fabric as is	

Purchase 3 skeins of 215 Apple Green and 2 skeins of 28 Myrtle. Buy 1 skein of each remaining color.

To find the starting point of the first cross-stitch: Measure across 4" from top left corner; measure downwards 3 1/8" from top left corner. Mark the point where these two measurements intersect. Start embroidering the top of the yellow bud in upper left corner.

Margin to be added when mounting: Add 1" borders on all four sides of the embroidery.

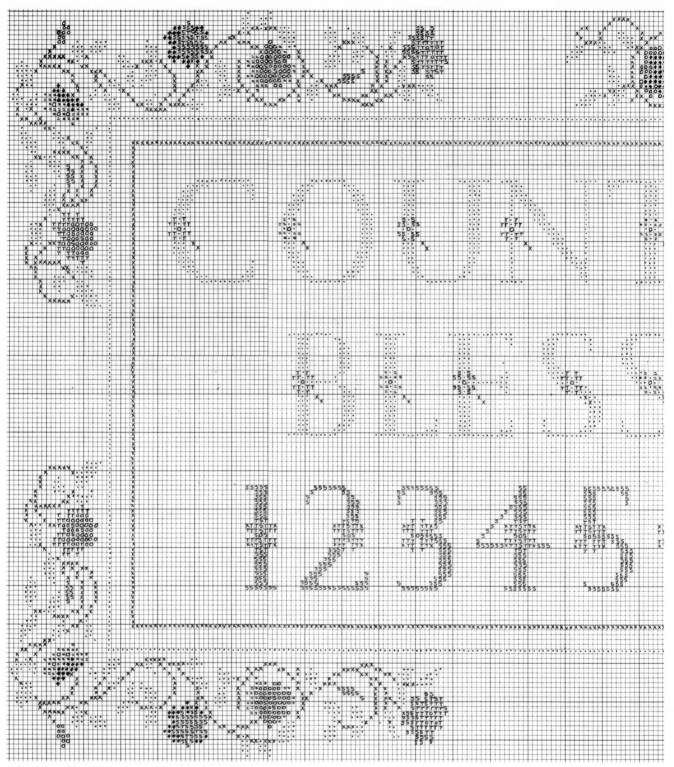

Illus. 69. Charted graph for "Count Your Blessings."

(Illus. 69 continued.)

God, Be Merciful to Me a Sinner

(Color page O)

Illus. 70.

Degree of work: moderate
Fabric: ivory aida (11 count)
Cut size of fabric needed: 26" wide x 17"
Finished size: approximately 21 3/4" x 12 7/8"

Cross-Stitch Color Key

Symbol	J. & P. Coats six-strand floss	or DMC six-strand floss
⊠	12 Black	310
·	36 Royal Purple	550
⊙	90A Bright Gold	783
⑤	Use DMC 414	414
③	109 Dk. Willow Green	367
■	61 Ecru	822
=	5A Chartreuse	704
☐	Fabric as is	

Backstitch Color Key

⊞	12 Black	310

Purchase 3 skeins each of 12 Black and 36 Royal Purple and 2 skeins each of 90A Bright Gold, DMC 414, 109 Dk. Willow Green, and 5A Chartreuse. Buy 1 skein of 61 Ecru.

To find the starting point of the first cross-stitch: Measure across 3" from top left corner; measure downwards 3" from top left corner. Mark the point where these two measurements intersect. Start embroidering the first black stitch at top left corner.

Area of backstitch (indicated by bold lines on charted graph): *12 Black*—all areas.

Margin to be added when mounting: Add 1" borders on all four sides of the embroidery.

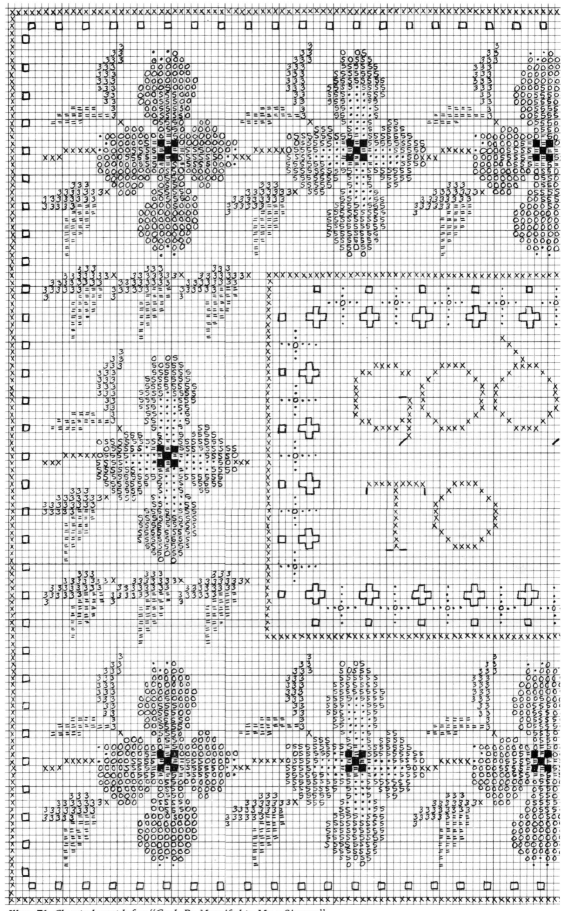

Illus. 71. Charted graph for "God, Be Merciful to Me a Sinner."

(Illus. 71 continued.)

(Illus. 71 continued.)

Come, Ye Thankful People (Color page O)

Degree of work: moderate
Fabric: ivory aida (11 count)
Cut size of fabric needed: 23" x 23"
Finished size: approximately 16 5/8" wide x 15 1/2"

Illus. 72.

Cross-Stitch Color Key

Symbol	J. & P. Coats six-strand floss	or DMC six-strand floss
⊠	81B Dk. Colonial Brown	801
S	62 Russet	435
–	140 Signal Red	321
Z	90A Bright Gold	783
C	99 Grass Green	703
■	1 White	Snow-White
◢	38 Dk. Orange	741
3	28B Treeleaf Green	991
·	5A Chartreuse	704
△	143 Lt. Cardinal	815
◿	75A Tropic Orange	920
♥	9 Yellow	745
▮	224 Nectarine	970
L	26 Nile Green	966
☐	Fabric as is	

Backstitch Color Key

⊞	143 Lt. Cardinal	815

Purchase 2 skeins each of 81B Dk. Colonial Brown and 140 Signal Red. Buy 1 skein of each remaining color.

To find the starting point of the first cross-stitch: Measure across 3" from top left corner; measure downwards 3" from top left corner. Mark the point where these two measurements intersect. Start embroidering the tip of the red triangle in top left corner of the design.

Areas of special concern: Change the signature line. See alphabet no. 4 and numerals no. 2. There are 148 spaces in width to work with (exact length of decorative line above the signature). Leave 1 space between each letter within a word and between each number within a date. Leave 4 spaces between each complete word and between word and date. Center the line.

Area of backstitch (indicated by bold lines on charted graph): *143 Lt. Cardinal*—all areas.

Margin to be added when mounting: Add 1 1/8" borders on all four sides of the embroidery.

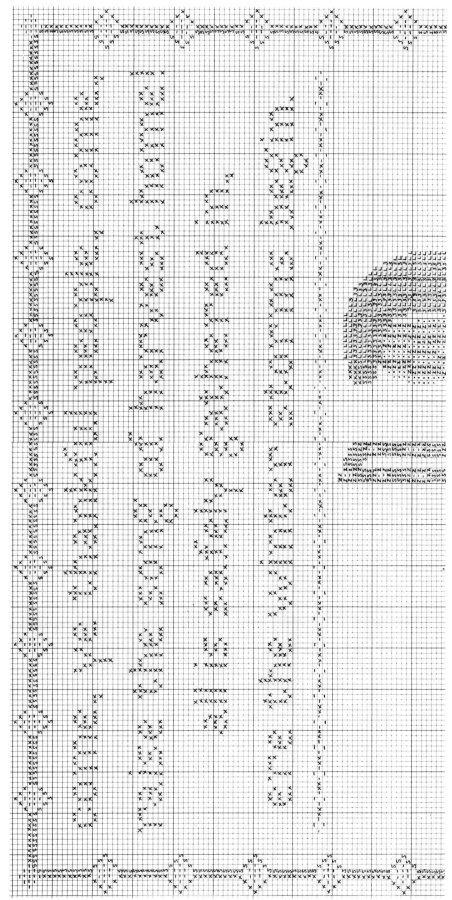

Illus. 73. Charted graph for "Come, Ye Thankful People."

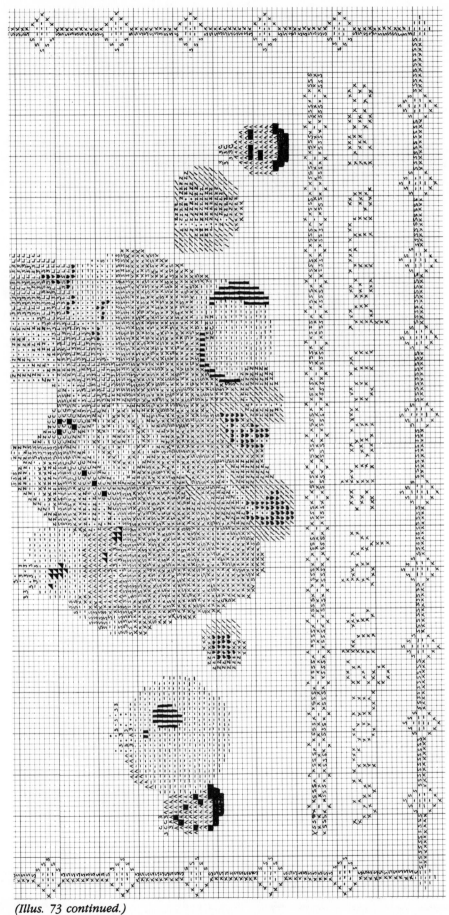

(Illus. 73 continued.)

He Who Is Faithful

(Color page P)

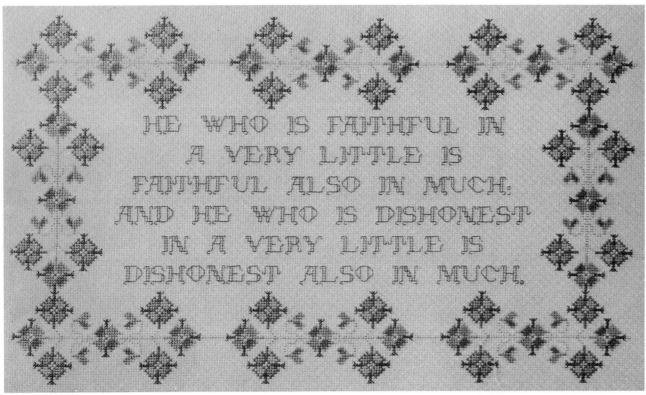

Illus. 74.

Degree of work: challenging
Fabric: white aida (11 count)
Cut size of fabric needed: 28" wide x 18"
Finished size: approximately 23 1/8" x 13 7/8"

Cross-Stitch Color Key

Symbol	J. & P. Coats six-strand floss	or DMC six-strand floss
⊠	75A Tropic Orange	920
•	26 Nile Green	966
S	81 Dk. Brown	434
U	260 Maple Wood	437
╱	69 Lt. Steel Blue	809
3	124 Indian Pink	353
☐	Fabric as is	

Backstitch Color Key

⊞	26 Nile Green	966
	81 Dk. Brown	434
	75A Tropic Orange	920

Purchase 2 skeins of 75A Tropic Orange. Buy 1 skein of each remaining color.

To find the starting point of the first cross-stitch: Measure across 4 1/2" from top left corner; measure downwards 3" from top left corner. Mark the point where these two measurements intersect. Start embroidering the first brown stitch at very top left side of design.

Areas of special concern: Watch spacing between 3 floral repeats at top and bottom. There are 10 spaces between the left and middle repeat, and there are 11 spaces between the middle and right repeats.

Area of backstitch (indicated by bold lines on charted graph): _26 Nile Green_—on stems connecting all flowers and buds. _81 Dk. Brown_—details on either side of brown areas on flowers. _75A Tropic Orange_—on entire verse.

Margin to be added when mounting: Add 7/8" borders on all four sides of the embroidery.

Illus. 75. Charted graph for "He Who Is Faithful."

FAITHFUL IN
LITTLE IS
SO IN MUCH:
IS DISHONEST
LITTLE IS
LSO IN MUCH.

(Illus. 75 continued.)

Roots and Wings

Illus. 76.

Degree of work: easy
Fabric: white aida (11 count)
Cut size of fabric needed: 27" wide x 19"
Finished size: approximately 21" x 13"

Cross-Stitch Color Key

Symbol	J. & P. Coats six-strand floss	or DMC six-strand floss
⊠	28 Myrtle	700
U	1 White	Snow-White
T	253 Daffodil	444
–	71 Pewter Grey	415
Q	98 Fern Green	989
3	143 Lt. Cardinal	815
e	91 Emerald Green	913
c	81 Dk. Brown	434
V	Use DMC 642	642
▲	12 Black	310
Z	124 Indian Pink	353
S	90A Bright Gold	783
O	75A Tropic Orange	920
M	109 Dk. Willow Green	367
⁄	5A Chartreuse	704
☐	Fabric as is	

Backstitch Color Key

	71 Pewter Grey	415
	28 Myrtle	700
	109 Dk. Willow Green	367
	81 Dk. Brown	434
	Use DMC 642	642
	12 Black	310

Buy 1 skein of each color.

To find the starting point of the first cross-stitch: Measure across 6 1/4" from the top left corner; measure downwards 4 1/8" from top left corner. Mark the point where these two measurements intersect. Start embroidering the tip of the topmost fern green leaf located behind white flower on the left side.

Area of backstitch (indicated by bold lines on charted graph): *71 Pewter Grey*—outline around two white flowers and inner lines as well. *28 Myrtle*—veins within three small petals on largest white flower; outline around small petals on shortest white flower; and veins in leaves of acorn plant. *109 Dk. Willow Green*—stems on buttercup. *81 Dk. Brown*—roots on buttercup and acorn plant. *DMC 642*—roots on two white flowers. *12 Black*—antennae and legs on butterfly resting on leaf; antennae, legs, and inner lines on butterfly hovering above word "but"; antennae on two butterflies on the right side of the sampler; and inner markings on two butterflies with Indian pink floss. *81 Dk. Brown*—antennae on butterfly hovering above the word "are."

Margin to be added when mounting: Add 3/4" borders on all four sides of the embroidery.

Illus. 77. Charted graph for "Roots and Wings."

(Illus. 77 continued.)

Alphabets and Numerals

Letters and numerals are made up of various parts. Some letters and numerals comprise only the main body, the space between the waist and base lines (Illus. 78); others include an upper stroke called the ascender (Illus. 79); and there are some that include a downward stroke called the descender (Illus. 80). Lowercase or small letters (Illus. 81) and uppercase or capital letters (Illus. 82) are also common terms of identification.

Since letters and numerals can vary so much in height, width, and thickness, and some distinctions are very fine, I have arranged my alphabets and numerals according to the height of the main body. For example, "five squares high" means that the main body of these small letters occupies five ver-

tical squares on the aida cloth. There may be ascenders and descenders, but the main area that each letter takes up is five squares or the equivalent of approximately 1/2" in height. If you create your own project and want taller lettering, say 1" in height, look through the alphabets that are approximately eleven squares high.

I charted complete cross-stitch alphabets and numerals in a wide variety of styles for you to use. These are assembled here with the names of samplers in which I used the letters and numerals. I hope you enjoy using the thirty-five alphabets and fifteen sets of numerals within my samplers. But why stop there? Use the charts to sign, date, and personalize original projects of your own.

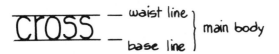

Illus. 78. Some letters occupy only one space, the "main body."

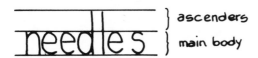

Illus. 79. Some letters have an upper stroke, the "ascender."

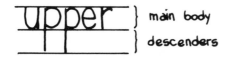

Illus. 80. Some letters have a downward stroke, the "descender."

Illus. 81. Non-capitals are lowercase letters.

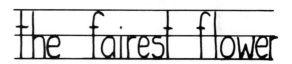

Illus. 82. Uppercase letters are known as capitals.

Alphabets

1. Four Squares High

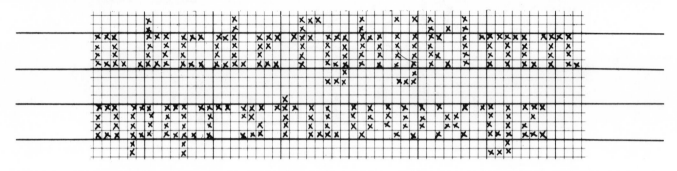

2. Five Squares High

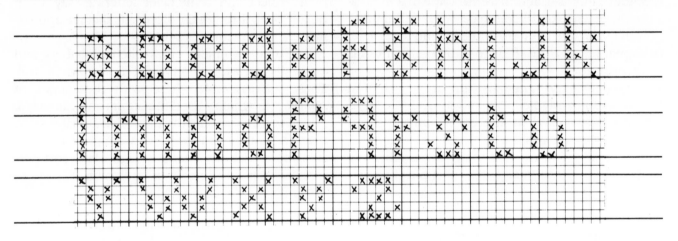

3. Five Squares High

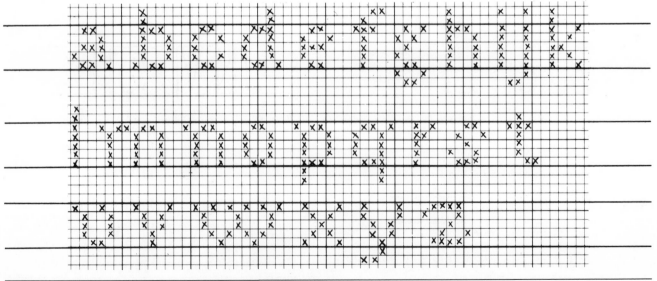

4. Five Squares High

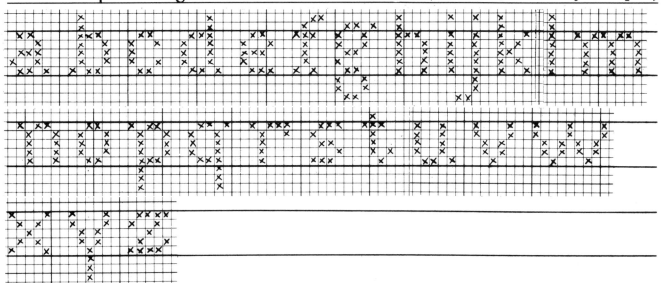

5. Five Squares High

(Cross-stitch and backstitch; two colors)

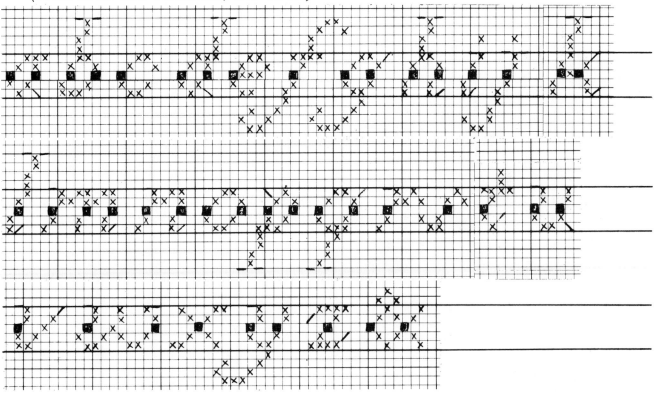

6. Five Squares High

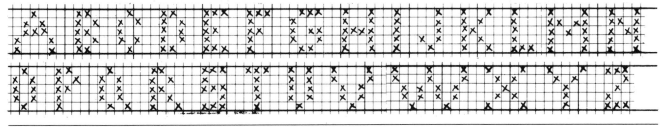

7. Six Squares High *(In "Teddy Bear")*

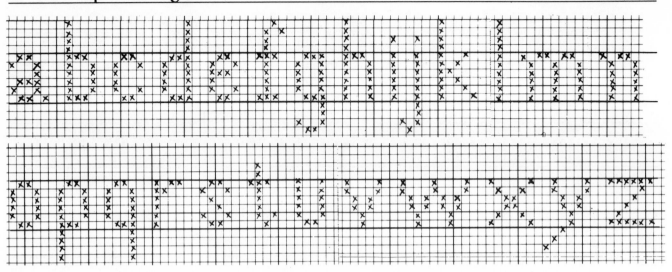

8. Six Squares High *(In "Happy Birthday")*
(Backstitch)

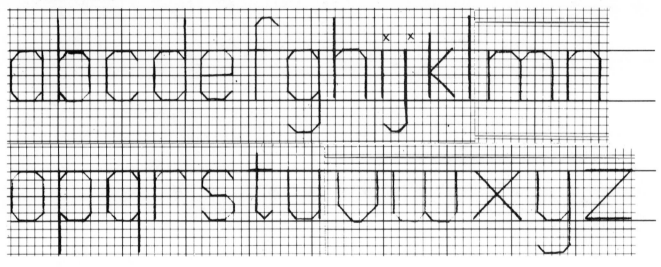

9. Six Squares High *(In "With This Ring I Thee Wed")*

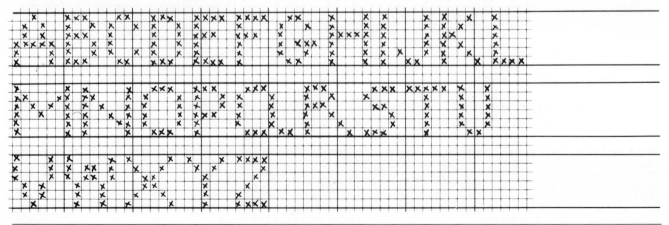

10. Six Squares High

(Backstitch)

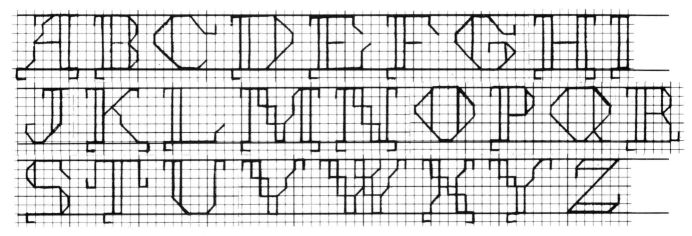

11. Seven Squares High

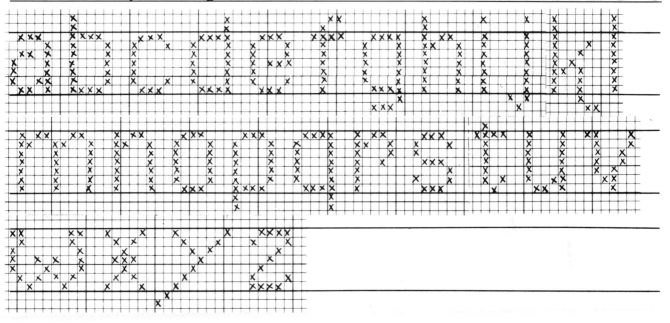

12. Seven Squares High

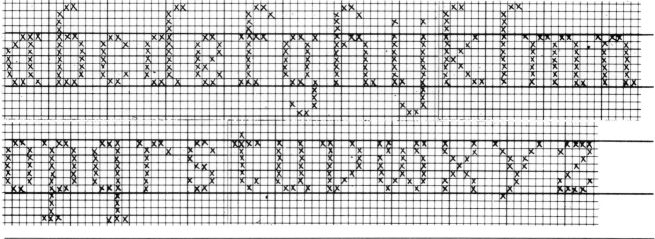

13. Seven Squares High *(In "Duck" and "Graduation")*

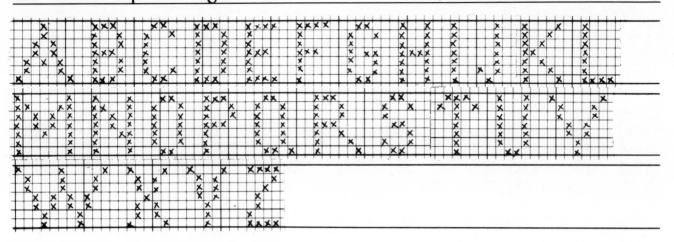

14. Seven Squares High *(In "Merry Christmas"
and "Roots and Wings")*

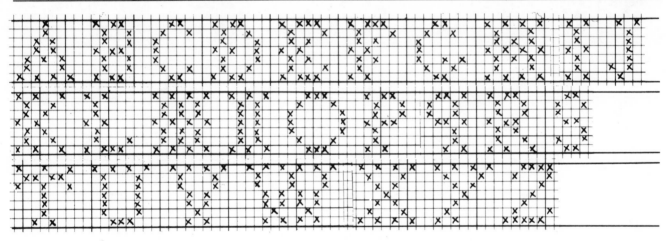

15. Seven Squares High *(In "Give Us Our Daily Bread")*

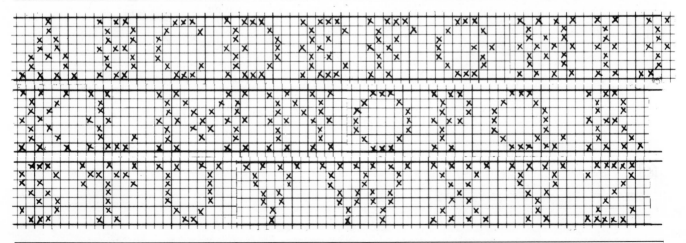

16. Seven Squares High

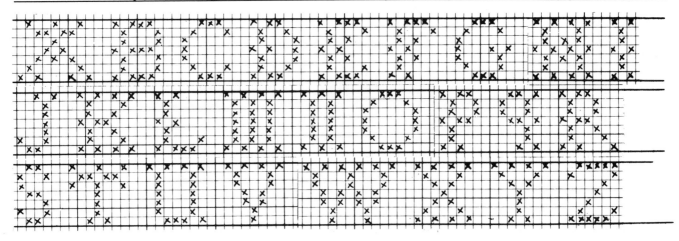

17. Seven Squares High

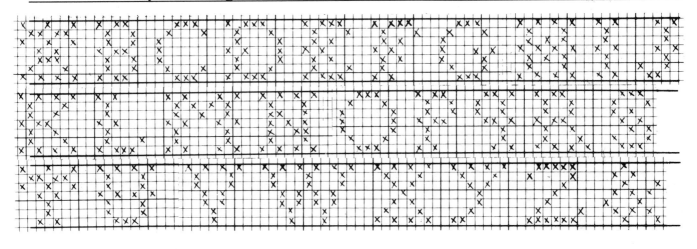

18. Eight Squares High

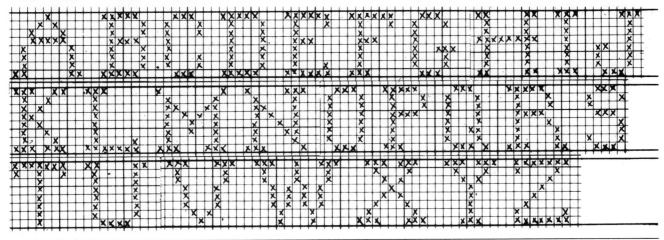

19. Eight Squares High
(Cross-stitch and backstitch)

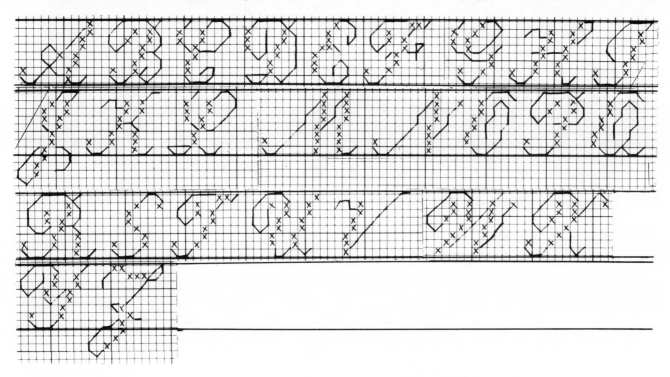

20. Nine Squares High

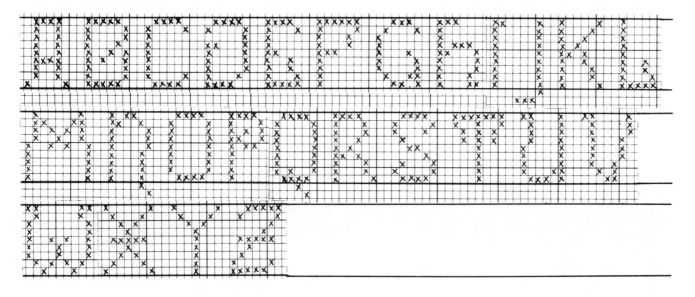

21. Nine Squares High

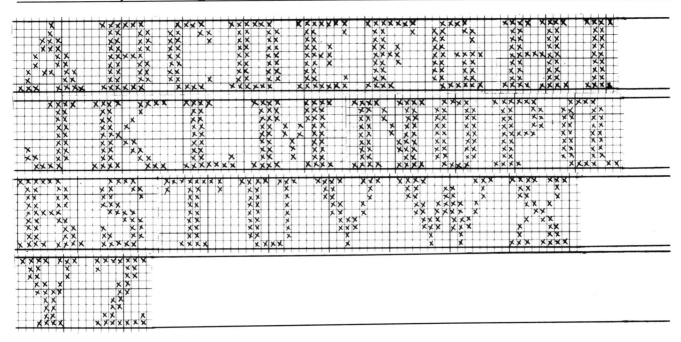

22. Ten Squares High
(Cross-stitch and backstitch)

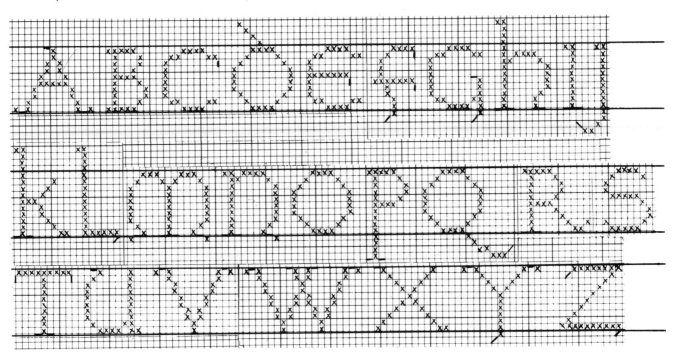

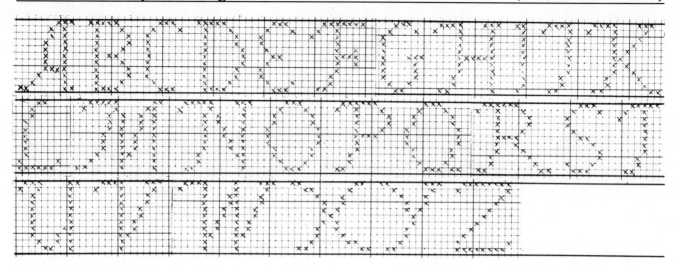

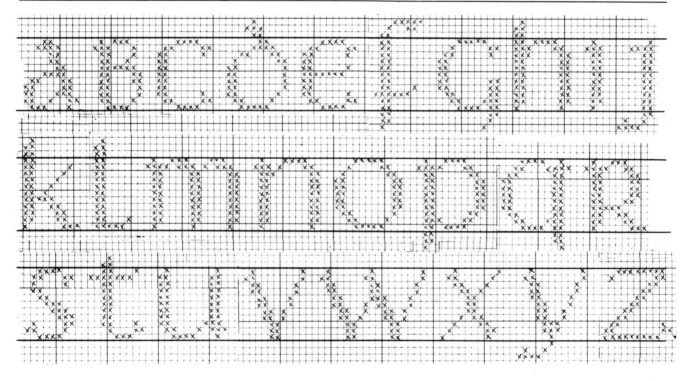

25. Eleven Squares High
(In "Town")

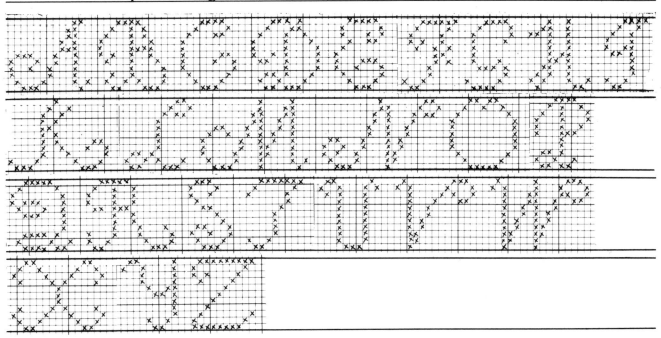

26. Eleven Squares High
(In "Happy Birthday" and "Merry Christmas")

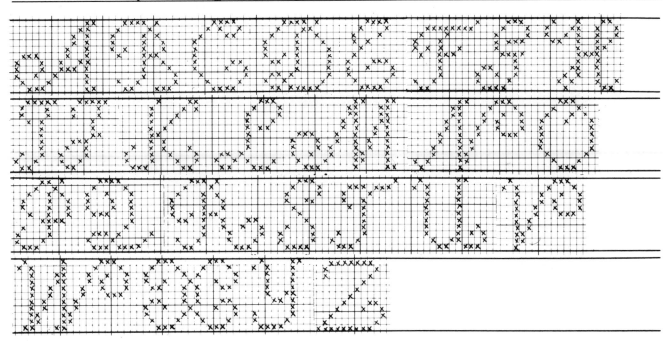

27. Twelve Squares High *(In "Teddy Bear" and "Flower Basket")*

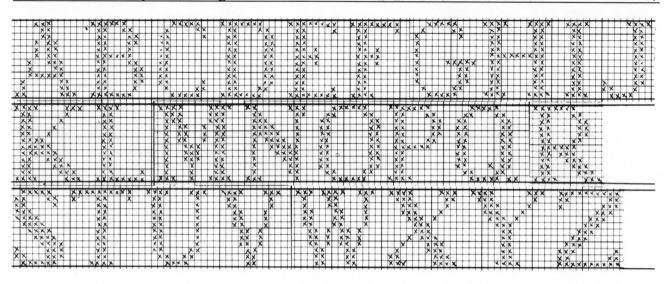

28. Twelve Squares High *(In "Love One Another")*

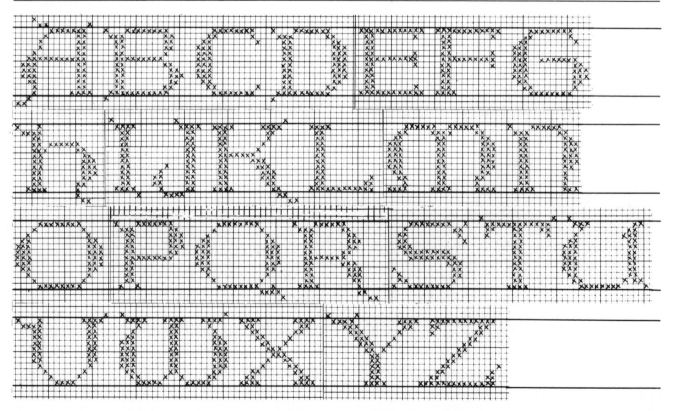

29. Twelve Squares High

(Three colors)

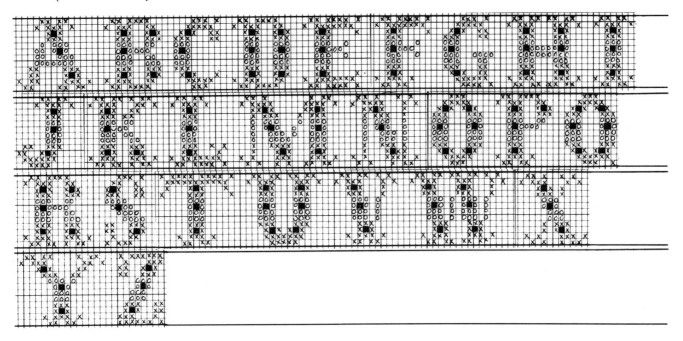

30. Thirteen Squares High

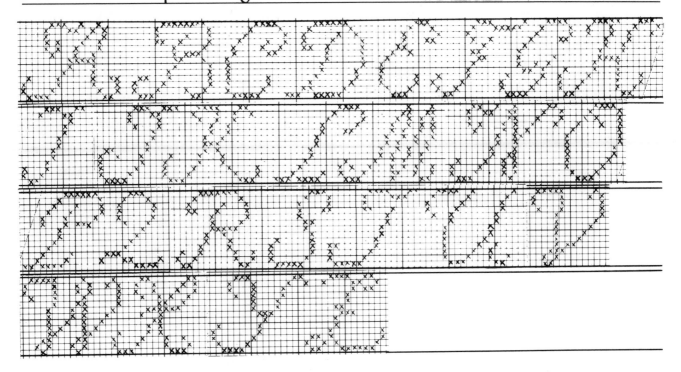

31. Fourteen Squares High

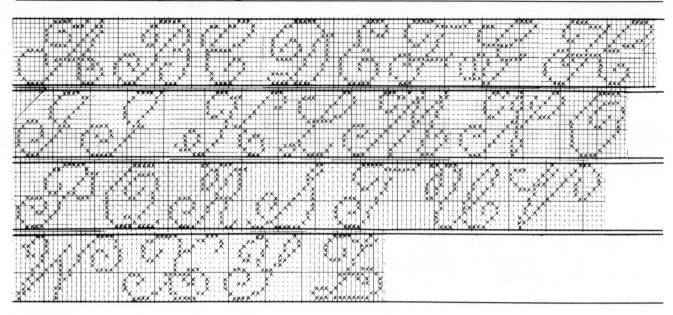

3 2. Fourteen Squares High
(Two colors)

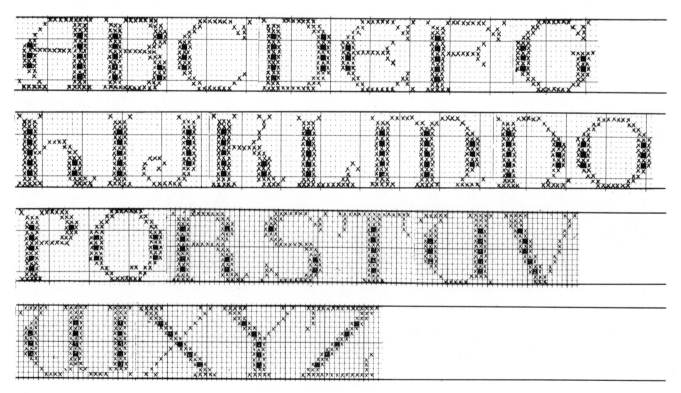

(Two colors)

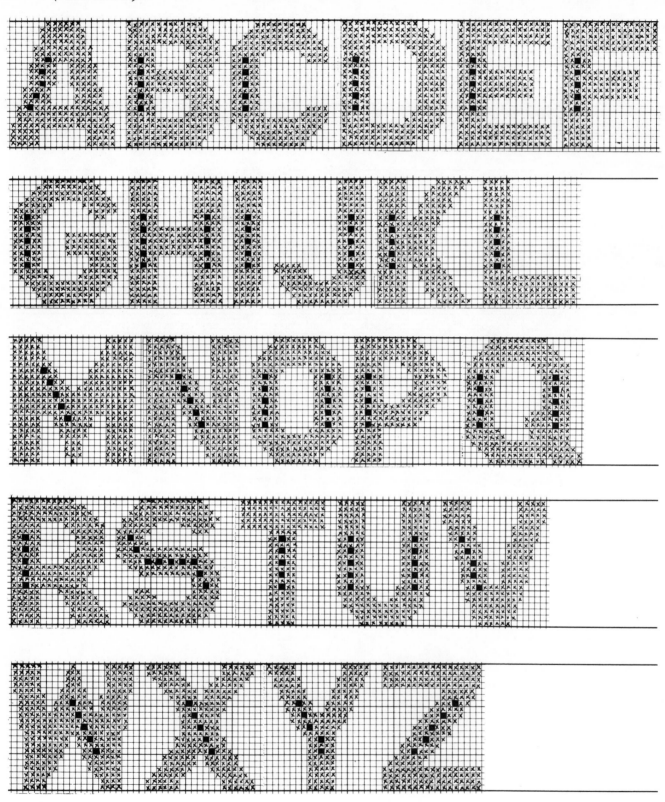

(Four colors)

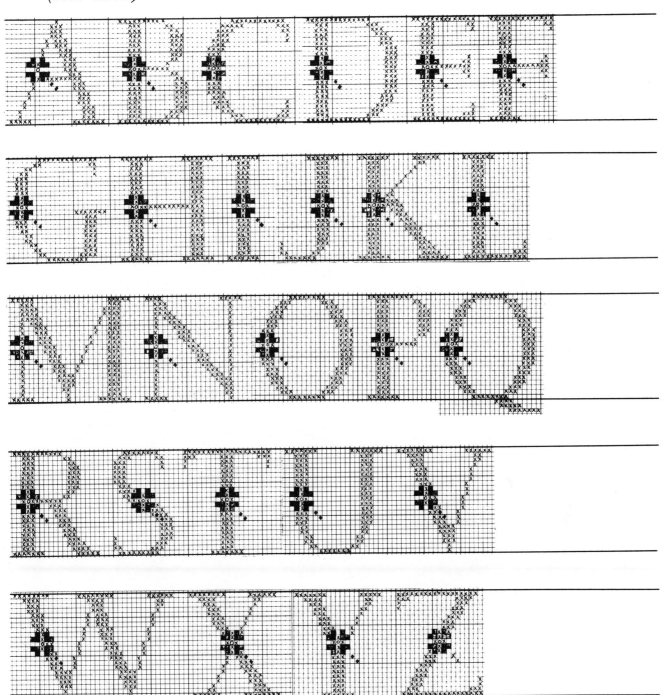

Numerals

1. Five Squares High   *(In "Family Register" and "Love One Another")*

2. Five Squares High   *(In "Come, Ye Thankful People")*

3. Five Squares High   *(In "Cupid")*

4. Five Squares High   *(In "Happy Anniversary")*

5. Six Squares High   *(In "With This Ring I Thee Wed")*

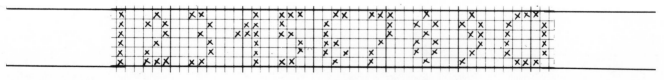

6. Six Squares High

(In "Teddy Bear")

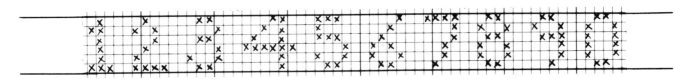

7. Seven Squares High

(In "Graduation,"
"Flower Basket," and "Give Us Our Daily Bread")

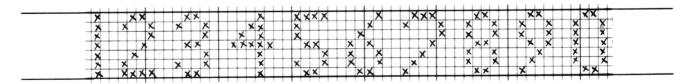

8. Seven Squares High

(In "Duck" and "In Loving Memory")

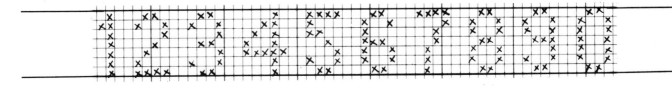

9. Seven Squares High

(In "Don't Count Your Chickens")

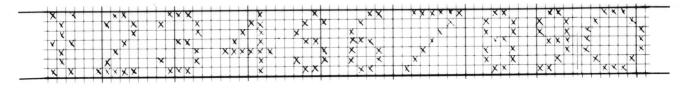

10. Seven Squares High

(In "Town")

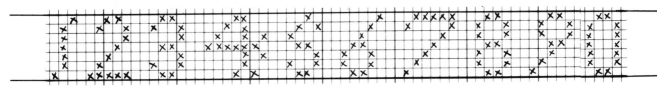

11. Seven Squares High   *(In "Swans" and "Merry Christmas")*

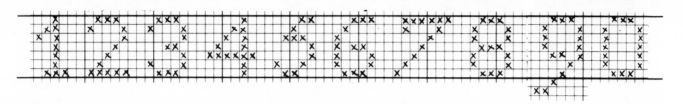

12. Nine Squares High   *(In "Flower Basket")*

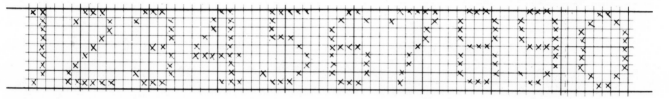

13. Ten Squares High   *(In "Happy Birthday")*

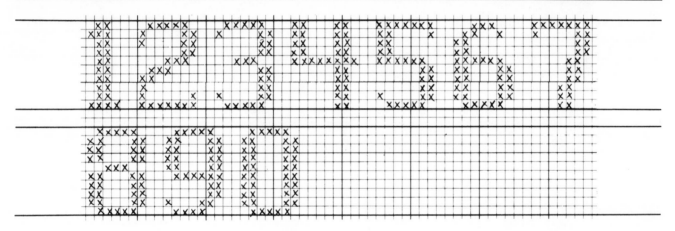

14. Eleven Squares High   *(In "Chipmunk among the Vegetables" and "Flower Basket")*

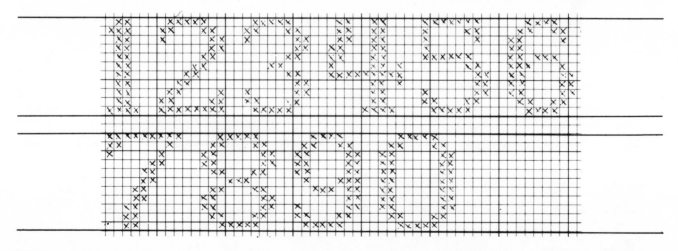

(Four colors)

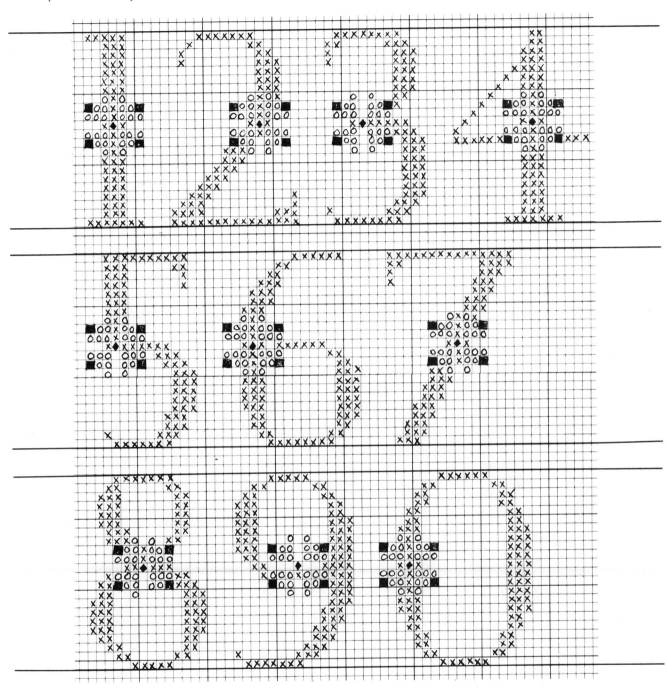

Index